PEER PRESSURE, PEER PREVENTION

Criminological research has largely neglected the possibility that positive peer influence is a potentially powerful source of social control. Quantitative methods tease out cause, effect, and spuriousness in the relationship between peer delinquency and personal delinquency, but do little or nothing to reveal *how and why* peers might influence each other toward—or away from—deviance.

Costello and Hope take a first step toward uncovering the mechanisms of peer influence, drawing on quantitative and qualitative data collected from two convenience samples of university students. Their quantitative analyses showed that positive or prosocial peer influence occurs most frequently among those who associate with the most deviant peers and self-report the most deviance, contrary to predictions drawn from social learning theories. Their qualitative data revealed a variety of methods of negative influence, including encouraging deviant behavior for others' amusement, a motive for peer influence never before reported in the literature.

Barbara J. Costello (Ph.D., University of Arizona) is Associate Professor of Sociology at the University of Rhode Island. Her research has focused on testing and extending control theories of crime and delinquency, and on the explanation of both positive and negative peer influence.

Trina L. Hope (Ph.D., University of Arizona) is Associate Professor of Sociology at the University of Oklahoma. Her research has focused primary on criminological theory-testing, including applying concepts from control theories to gang membership, gang and dating violence, adolescent sexual activity, pregnancy resolution, and substance use.

PEER PRESSURE, PEER PREVENTION

"This is an original effort to calm long-standing squabbles among criminologists about the place of peers in explanations of deviant acts. Costello and Hope see that these disputes—fueled by deductive theory and statistical analyses—may be resolved by quietly questioning people performing and reacting to the acts in question. Their findings justify their effort. All is not as we have been led to believe. The several claimants to this disputed territory—whether strain, control, or learning theorists—will find good reasons to rethink their claims. Need I note that such progress is rare?"
                                    —Travis Hirschi, Emeritus Professor of Sociology, University of Arizona

"This book makes a major contribution by considering how peer pressure goes in multiple directions. It broadens our discussion of peer effects on crime and thus can help resolve many of the issues that have been discussed for many decades."
                                    —Marcus Felson, Professor of Sociology, Texas State University

"Criminologists know little more about mechanisms of peer influence or the everyday social interaction of youth than they did a generation ago. This is a sad and startling admission, particularly in light of all the attention that peer influence has received in recent years. This book brings the authority and richness of real life back into the study of peer influence, along with an abundance of original insights and ideas. For an area often hindered by methodological controversies and theoretical inertia, this should be welcome news. Costello and Hope deserve our thanks."
                                    —Mark Warr, Professor of Sociology, University of Texas at Austin

PEER PRESSURE, PEER PREVENTION

The Role of Friends in Crime and Conformity

Barbara J. Costello and Trina L. Hope

Routledge
Taylor & Francis Group

NEW YORK AND LONDON

First published 2016
by Routledge
711 Third Avenue, New York, NY 10017

and by Routledge
2 Park Square, Milton Park, Abingdon, Oxon, OX14 4RN

Routledge is an imprint of the Taylor & Francis Group, an informa business

Library of Congress Cataloging-in-Publication Data
Names: Costello, Barbara J. | Hope, Trina L.
Title: Peer pressure, peer prevention : the role of friends in crime and conformity / Barbara J. Costello & Trina L. Hope.
Description: New York : Routledge, 2016. | Includes bibliographical references and index.
Identifiers: LCCN 2015037697| ISBN 9781138951709 (hbk. : alk. paper) |
    ISBN 9781138951693 (pbk. : alk. paper) | ISBN 9781315668055 (ebk.)
Subjects: LCSH: Conformity. | Peer pressure. | Influence (Psychology) | Criminology.
Classification: LCC HM1246 .C67 2016 | DDC 303.3/2—dc23
LC record available at http://lccn.loc.gov/2015037697

ISBN: 978-1-138-95170-9 (hbk)
ISBN: 978-1-138-95169-3 (pbk)
ISBN: 978-1-315-66805-5 (ebk)

Typeset in Bembo
by Apex CoVantage, LLC

CONTENTS

PREFACE

The idea for this book came out of my reading of the literature on peer influence processes. Given my background as a student of Travis Hirschi and Michael Gottfredson at the University of Arizona, I began my career skeptical of explanations of peer influence that relied on peers teaching each other that deviant behavior is okay or good. My background as a teenager who engaged in some minor delinquent acts also left me skeptical of explanations that held that youths commit crime because they don't see anything wrong with it—my friends and I were well aware that the mischief we were up to was not right, not acceptable under the circumstances, and that we'd be in a lot of trouble if we got caught. There was nothing in the literature on peer influence that convinced me that my skepticism was misguided. Further, it struck me that criminologists studying peer influence tended to overlook one obvious fact—youths engage in conforming behavior together at least as much as they engage in deviance together. In fact, I noted this point in my first professional publication (Costello 1997).

I became more interested in studying peer influence as social network analysis came to be used extensively in criminology. I attended an excellent course in social network analysis taught by Stanley Wasserman and Bernice Pescosolido at Indiana University. I learned a lot about network analysis in the course, including the fact that it simply couldn't answer the questions that I thought were key in the study of peer influence. Network analysis can reveal a great deal about the structure of social groups and how attitudes and behaviors are connected among group members, but what it can't do is tell us much about how peer influence plays out on the micro-level. If a behavior "spreads" across members of a group over time, how and why does that happen? This is the question of causal mechanism that I think has remained unanswered despite advances in quantitative methods in sociology and criminology.

I started asking my students at the University of Rhode Island (URI) questions about their experiences with peer influence, and collected some preliminary data from them in the form of papers written for my classes. I realized that student papers were a great source of data that required few resources to collect, and in Fall 2009 I formally collected data in the form of anonymous papers written by my students in a large General Sociology course I was teaching. I realized that quantitative data would be a great addition to the qualitative data I had, and I asked my friend and graduate school colleague Trina Hope if she would be interested and able to collect some data at the University of Oklahoma (OU) for a collaborative project. With an eye primarily toward positive peer influence, we designed and administered a questionnaire to a small sample of URI students and a larger sample of OU students, and also collected additional qualitative data from both samples. Although our sample cannot be assumed to be representative of students at these universities, we ended up with a rich data set including both qualitative and quantitative measures of peer influence processes.[1]

This book is intended to be a first step in uncovering the reasons behind the peer effect on deviance, in other words, to explain why there is a relationship between the individuals' deviance and that of their peers. It is also intended to expand sociologists' and criminologists' focus on peer influence to include positive peer pressure, or the tendency of people to discourage deviance among their friends and to encourage productive, prosocial behaviors that promote health and wellbeing. We approach both questions from a theoretical perspective that has long discounted the importance of direct peer influence on behavior, and take a fresh look at peer influence from a control theory perspective.

Our respondents have told us in their own words about their experiences with both positive and negative peer influence, both on the "giving" and "receiving" ends of the interactions. In addition to the unprecedented look at influence processes this has provided us, we think our presentation of these data will make our book accessible to undergraduate students, who might recognize themselves or their friends in some of our students' accounts. The book might also spark some interesting ideas for student research projects. Students might collect their own data on peer influence among their friends, roommates, or fraternity brothers and sorority sisters. Some of our respondents mentioned posting videos of their antics on YouTube, which led us to wonder what a systematic analysis of YouTube videos might turn up. It might also be interesting to analyze peer influence processes in movies and novels—we've noticed a number of references to positive peer influence processes in the *Harry Potter* books and movies, for example. We hope using this book in our own courses will lead students to give us new ideas for future research projects as well.

We also think that this book will be of value to anyone interested in peer influence processes or criminological theory in general. Scholars in criminology, sociology, psychology, the study of drug and alcohol use, and adolescent behavior should find our book useful. We briefly touch on implications of our findings for policy as well, and we hope that our findings can inform programs designed to prevent behaviors that often involve bystanders, such as bullying, sexual assault among college and university students, and drug and alcohol abuse. Prevention programs should be grounded in the findings of basic research, drawing on what we know about what peers actually do to intervene in each other's deviance, and on what we know about when they are likely to be successful.

Note

1. We are happy to share our data with interested researchers upon request.

ACKNOWLEDGMENTS

Funding for preliminary phases of this research was provided to the first author by the URI Foundation. Funding for data collection at the University of Oklahoma was provided by the department of Sociology at OU.

We thank the many colleagues who have provided feedback on various stages of this project. We especially thank those who read and provided extensive feedback on the full manuscript: Travis Hirschi, Bianca Bersani, Holly Dunsworth, and Craig St. John. Other colleagues who provided feedback and suggestions on parts of the manuscript in its various stages include: Brad Anderson, Leo Carroll, Connie Chapple, Marcus Felson, C. B. Peters, and Mark Warr.

At Routledge, thanks to Steve Rutter for his encouragement in the early stages of bringing this book to publication, and thanks to Pamela Chester and Irene Bunnell.

1

INTRODUCTION

The Study of Peers and Deviant Behavior

Sometimes kids get into trouble. Kids get into more trouble when they're around their friends than when they're alone. Parents often react to kids getting into trouble with friends by forbidding them to hang around with those friends, arguing that they're a "bad influence." But are they? And if so, exactly how does that influence happen? If we knew the answer to these questions, we'd be in a much better position to try to prevent delinquent, deviant, or criminal behavior before it happens.

On the other hand, kids can keep each other out of trouble. We're all familiar with the catch phrase, "Friends don't let friends drive drunk." Do they, or don't they? Surprisingly, we know very little about "positive peer pressure," including how often it happens, when it happens, who does it, and whether or not it works. If we knew the answer to these questions, we would be in a better position to encourage peer interference with deviant behaviors, and to encourage peers to influence each other towards a range of positive, productive behaviors.

These two issues are the focus of this book. Social scientists have known for decades what parents have known for thousands of years—that kids get into more trouble when they're with other kids. But we have not done a very good job of finding out why. We know that there is a lot of truth to the adage, "Birds of a feather flock together," or the idea that people who are alike in some important respect tend to come together and become friends. This is the process of self-selection, which explains that friendship groups do not form randomly, but rather that people with similar preferences tend to get together. But beyond that, we know very little about exactly what happens in the context of friendship groups that seems to promote bad behavior. The number of possible explanations for the correlation between having deviant friends and engaging in delinquent or criminal behavior is large, and includes the following possibilities, which we refer to throughout the book as *causal mechanisms* that can explain the correlation:

Friends can:

- Teach norms and values that promote deviant behavior
- Reward deviant behavior by providing an appreciative audience
- Make suggestions for deviant acts or provide opportunities for deviance, such as offering/supplying drugs or alcohol

- Model deviant behavior that can be imitated by their friends
- Teach friends how to engage in deviant behavior
- Ridicule others who are reluctant to engage in deviant or risky behavior
- Dare friends to engage in deviant or risky behavior
- Minimize individual responsibility by sharing in the activity
- Make the activity more fun, because doing things with friends is more fun than doing things alone
- Repeatedly ask or "badger" friends into engaging in deviance
- Convince reluctant friends they won't get caught
- Threaten to end a friendship if a friend won't engage in deviance with them
- Act as "lookouts" or accomplices to make deviant behavior easier, more rewarding, or easier to get away with
- Act as buyers for stolen goods or drugs

All of these possibilities, and more, have been suggested in the literature on peers and delinquency. We simply do not know which of these is most common or most important, in part because existing data sets do not allow us to determine why we see commonalities in friends' behavior, and why delinquency tends to occur in groups. To address this gap in the literature, we simply asked young people to tell us what happens when they're with their friends. This straightforward approach has revealed some important insights into peer influence on deviant behavior, which we present in Chapter 3.

Our other major focus in this book is on the process of positive peer influence, which can be of two types. Friends can prevent each other from engaging in deviant or criminal behavior, as when someone stops a drunk person from driving. They can also encourage positive behaviors, such as studying, beginning an exercise program, or eating more healthfully. The field of criminology has for too long focused on how peers can cause delinquent or deviant behavior, and has largely overlooked the possibility that peers can also have positive influences on each other's behavior. In addition to asking our respondents how their friends influence their deviant behavior, then, we also asked them to tell us how they and their friends prevent deviance or promote positive behaviors in one another. We present our analysis of their descriptions of these events in Chapter 4.

In Chapter 5 we move from qualitative data to a quantitative analysis of the factors that predict how often peers try to influence each other's behavior in a positive direction, which types of individuals are most likely to engage in such attempts at positive influence, and when they are likely to be successful. We present our analysis of several hypotheses derived from control theories of crime (Gottfredson and Hirschi 1990; Hirschi 1969), focusing on how social control and self-control processes can operate in peer groups to prevent deviant behavior. While some of our findings were consistent with what we expected, some were surprising, and perhaps even more interesting.

We begin in Chapter 2 by presenting an overview of existing theory and research on peer influence. We review a number of different bodies of literature, including theory and research on learning theories of crime, control theories of crime, research on children's friendships that has primarily been conducted by psychologists, social network analysis, and research in criminology that has studied the nature of friendships among delinquent or deviant individuals compared to non-deviant people. Our focus in this chapter is on alternatives to learning theories, which have dominated the literature on peers and delinquency. We show that despite good evidence that peer influence does not work primarily through peers teaching each other that crime is okay (Warr 2002), the literature often simply assumes that peer influence operates through learning processes. This has led criminologists to neglect other possibilities, which we explore throughout the book.

We know that the questions we seek to answer are important, and that they have not been systematically addressed by prior research in the field of criminology. While taking on new questions is an exciting prospect, it also comes with challenges—namely, how do we actually answer these crucial questions? What kind of data should we collect, and what questions should we ask? We decided to start with the simple, inexpensive, and obvious, using respondents we know well and have access to—our students. We began our data collection by simply asking students at the University of Rhode Island (URI) to write about incidents they participated in that involved peer influence toward both positive or conforming behavior and negative or deviant behavior. Later, we conducted surveys at URI and at the University of Oklahoma (UO) that asked students about a wide range of peer influence attempts, in addition to their demographic characteristics, a range of attitudes, and their own behavior, with a particular focus on attempts at positive peer pressure.

Thanks to the willingness of our students to participate, we were able to collect data from over 800 respondents. Although our sampling technique was not meant to produce a representative sample of American undergraduate students, it does closely resemble the undergraduate populations of URI and OU, as discussed further in Chapter 5. Compared to American college students as a whole, our sample is less racially diverse (30% of our sample chose at least one non-white racial category, while non-whites comprise about 40% of U.S. undergraduates), and a bit younger (75% of our sample is 21 or younger, vs. 54% of U.S. undergrads). Similar to the population of undergraduates as a whole, however, 59% of our sample is female (vs. 57% for undergrads nationally).

Our sample has both strengths and weaknesses. One important limitation of our sample is that it cannot be assumed to be representative of young people or of college students in general. We cannot know whether our results will be replicated in studies on other college or university campuses, and we also cannot know whether the patterns we have found will be similar among a non-student sample of the same age. The second major limitation of our sample is that we would expect a college student sample to be less deviant than samples of either younger people as a whole or those who do not attend college. Persistence in education is not a typical characteristic of serious offenders, and commitment to educational goals is consistently found to be associated with lower levels of delinquency/crime (Gottfredson and Hirschi 1990; Hirschi 1969). Thus, it is possible that our results are different than they would be for more serious or higher-rate offenders.

On the other hand, there is no lack of deviant or criminal behavior among college students. Alcohol and drug abuse on college campuses has been of great concern to both social researchers and the public for many years. A recent search on Google Scholar using the terms "alcohol" and "college student" turned up over 171,000 studies published in the last ten years (Google Scholar website, July 21, 2015). Sexual assault on college campuses has also become a serious concern, with nearly 29,000 scholarly publications in the past ten years (Google Scholar website, July 21, 2015). In January 2014, President Obama created the White House Task Force to Protect Students from Sexual Assault (www.notalone.gov/), further demonstrating the importance of the problem in this population. In terms of overall crime victimization, one study of college student victimization found that about one-quarter of students reported being the victim of a crime on campus in one academic year (Fisher, Sloan, Cullen, and Lu 1998).

In addition, for most students, the college years are the first experience youths have away from their parents' home, and for many of them it is a time of experimentation with a variety of new behaviors. Freedom from the daily supervision of parents, in combination with a social environment comprised almost entirely of other youths of the same age, presents great opportunity for initiating a variety of new behaviors, both conforming and deviant.

Although our sample has weaknesses in terms of generalizability, in some ways college students are an ideal population to study to learn more about peer influence. They are away from parental supervision for probably the first time in their lives, they are surrounded by peers of the same age and life stage, and they are known to engage in and be victimized by a variety of deviant and criminal behaviors. Because our study is a first step in learning more about the mechanisms of peer influence, we believe the flaws in our sample are outweighed by the insights we've gained from our study.

2

THEORY AND RESEARCH ON PEERS AND DEVIANCE

The Peer Delinquency/Delinquency Connection

The focus on delinquent peers as a possible cause of delinquent behavior has its roots in two empirical facts: delinquent youth tend to have delinquent friends, and much delinquent behavior occurs in groups. From the very beginnings of the sociological study of delinquency (Shaw 1931; Shaw and McKay 1942; Sutherland 1947), the group nature of delinquency and the tendency for delinquency to cluster in certain neighborhoods has been posited as important in delinquency causation. Empirical research has continued to find that delinquency is largely a group phenomenon, with some deviant behaviors such as drug use and vandalism occurring almost exclusively in groups (Warr 2002).

Despite decades of research on this issue, there are two major questions that have yet to be answered. First, what are the mechanisms by which peers influence each other's behavior toward crime and deviance? That is, if peers do have a causal influence on each other's behavior, exactly *how* does that happen? As Warr (2002: 134) notes in his book *Companions in Crime*, a mere correlation between peer and individual deviance ". . . says nothing about the process or mechanism of influence that gave rise to it, and the number of possibilities is large . . ." There has been no research that explicitly examines those processes by simply asking people to report on exactly what happens in peer interactions preceding deviance. That is the approach we take in this work.

The second major question that has not yet been answered in the criminological literature, or really even addressed in any significant way, is whether and to what extent peers can have a positive influence on each other's behavior. The field of criminology has long considered the question, "What causes crime?" to be more important than "What causes conformity?" However, from our perspective, it is possible and likely that peers exert "positive peer pressure" on each other just as they may exert pressure or other forms of influence toward deviance. Working from a control theory perspective (Gottfredson and Hirschi 1990; Hirschi [1969] 2002), we investigate the extent to which peers influence each other's behavior in a prosocial direction, and the methods they use to do so.

The literature on peers and deviance has been dominated by learning theories of crime, with the major alternative explanation of the correlation between individual and peer delinquency being self-selection, the argument favored by control theorists. We describe these two perspectives below.

Learning Theories

The vast majority of explanations of delinquency focusing on delinquent peers draw on the idea that crime and delinquency are learned from others. This idea is an old one, and can be traced back at least as far as the Greek dramatist Thais, who in around 300 bc wrote, "bad company corrupts good character" (also translated as "evil companionships corrupt good morals," as cited in Burt 1925: 123). It is not surprising, then, that some of the earliest works on the causes of crime also draw on this idea. Even Cesare Lombroso, most closely associated with the idea that crime has biological roots, thought that some crimes were the result of imitation, and that a "depraved environment, which counsels or even insists on wrongdoing, and the bad example of parents or relatives" are "sinister" influences on children (Lombroso-Ferrero 1911: 144). Shaw and McKay argued that socially disorganized communities allow delinquent traditions to flourish, stating that delinquency is "part of the culture and tradition which is transmitted through the medium of social contact" in high crime neighborhoods (Shaw 1931: 18). However, the notion that crime is learned is most closely associated with the work of Edwin Sutherland (1947), who argued that crime is learned through association with others who teach "definitions favorable to violation of law," or in other words, norms that promote criminal behavior (Sutherland, Cressey, and Luckenbill 1992: 89). Later, Burgess and Akers (1966) explicitly incorporated the language of learning theory into Sutherland's theory, arguing that deviant behavior is learned through the process of reinforcement for deviant behavior and deviant verbalizations.

Sutherland's differential association theory and Akers's differential association-reinforcement theory are based on the idea that everyone has some contact with deviant and conforming others; those of us who have more contact with deviant others will be exposed to "an excess of definitions favorable to violation of law" (Sutherland, Cressey, and Luckenbill 1992: 89), or will experience greater reinforcement for deviant behavior than for non-deviant behavior (Burgess and Akers 1966). These theories hold that the dominant culture in a society may condemn crime, but at the same time there are deviant subcultures that have their own values in opposition to those of the dominant culture. Although Sutherland noted that some of what's learned in the process of learning criminal behavior is techniques for committing crime, the emphasis in both his and Akers's theory is on learning norms or definitions that support criminal behavior. As Kornhauser (1978) summarized it, criminal behavior for cultural deviance theories such as Sutherland's and Akers's is normal learned behavior—people do not violate the norms of their own subculture, they only violate norms of the dominant culture.

For learning theories, then, crime and deviance are social. They have social causes in that they are learned from others in the process of social interaction, and the strength of our ties to others affects the learning process. Sutherland held that associations that are greater in "frequency, duration, priority, and intensity" will be more likely to affect norms and behavior. In other words, people we come into contact with more often, for longer periods of time, earlier in life, and those with whom we have closer relationships will have a greater impact on our behavior. For Akers, these aspects of associations are important because they can affect the likelihood that we will experience reinforcement for deviant behavior (Akers 1998). Given their focus on the social causes of crime, it seems only natural that learning theories have dominated the literature on the peer–delinquency connection. However, this perspective has been challenged, often from theorists working in the control theory tradition (Costello 1997; Hirschi 1969; Kornhauser 1978). Control theories hold that the causes of crime are asocial, simply the result of people's desires to maximize pleasure and minimize pain. For control theories, social ties *prevent* crime rather than cause it, and thus the peer group is not seen as an important cause of crime. We summarize the key issues in the debate between learning and control theories below.

Self-Selection and Control Theories versus Learning Theories

Despite the dominance of cultural deviance or learning theories in the explanation of the peer delinquency/delinquency connection, critiques of these explanations are almost as old as the explanations themselves. As Burt (1925: 123–4) stated:

> Of all the explanations offered to the investigator for the wrongdoing of a particular child, the commonest is the influence of bad companions. This, naturally, is the preferred suggestion of the pained and anxious parent: each boy's mother blames some other mother's son. It is an excuse which, just because its working seems so clear and so intelligible, should never be too hastily accepted as the sole and self-sufficient reason for an offense.

The most commonly cited alternative to learning explanations of the peer delinquency/delinquency connection is self-selection, or the idea that the correlation between peer delinquency and delinquency is spurious, and not a causal relationship at all. First popularized in criminology by the Gluecks (Glueck and Glueck 1950), the phrase "birds of a feather flock together" neatly summarizes the idea that people with similar tendencies or interests will tend to seek each other out, a process often referred to as homophily[1]. The Gluecks referred to the process of selection as a "fundamental fact" and dismissed the idea that "accidental differential association of non-delinquents with delinquents is the basic cause of crime" (1950: 164.)

There is substantial evidence that self-selection is, in fact, an important cause of the similarity in peers' levels of delinquency. Kandel (1978) found that about 50% of the variance in similarity between friends was explained by self-selection. Cairns and Cairns found that self-selection was a major source of similarity in friendship groups on a number of demographic characteristics, and concluded from their study that both self-selection and socialization or "contagion" explain behavioral similarity between friends (1994: 177). Many recent studies find that selection processes play a large role in explaining similarity in friends' behavior, some of which find that self-selection is more important than friends' influence (Chapple 2005; Haynie and Osgood 2005; Matsueda and Anderson 1998; Mercken et al. 2010; Rebellon 2012).

In modern criminology, this idea that self-selection is responsible for the connection between delinquency and peer delinquency is most closely associated with control theory (Gottfredson and Hirschi 1990; Hirschi [1969] 2002). Travis Hirschi's social control theory (1969) holds that crime and delinquency are the result of a weak bond to society. If we are not emotionally attached to others, we do not care what others think of us and are therefore free to commit crime. If we have little or no investment in educational goals or an occupation, we have little to lose and are free to commit crime. Like the classical school of criminology and philosophers such as Hobbes, Hirschi assumed that crime comes naturally, as it provides a way for us to get what we want more quickly and more easily than conventional means. Control theories thus begin with the assumption that crime does not need to be learned, and in fact conformity, not crime, is in need of explanation. Why don't more of us commit crime more often? For Hirschi, it's because most of us have too much to lose to make crime worth the risk.

Social control theory also argues that it is not possible for a social group to hold norms that favor or even allow criminal or delinquent behavior (Hirschi 1969). Because crime often provides rewards for the offender at the expense of those with whom he or she associates, no social group can both maintain order and tolerate or promote crime. As Kornhauser put it, "There is no culture known to man in which those actions enjoined in the core of the criminal law are or can be collectively endowed with value, for they have no value for human beings whose existence depends upon their safe association with one another" (1978: 244). Thus, control theory denies the existence of deviant subcultures, or groups that value or promote crime among their members. Those who are more closely tied to any social group, then, will be more bound by the norms and laws of that group than those with weak ties. As Durkheim put it, "We are moral beings to the extent that we are social beings" (cited in Hirschi 1969: 18). Our ties to others are not criminogenic; on the contrary, they promote conformity.

The assumptions from which Hirschi (1969) began were retained in Hirschi's later work with Michael Gottfredson in *A General Theory of Crime* (Gottfredson and Hirschi 1990). In this work Gottfredson and Hirschi argue that the main cause of crime is low self-control. Put briefly, low self-control is the tendency to act impulsively without adequate consideration of the long-term consequences of behavior, both for the individual him- or herself, and for the individual's friends, family members, or others (Gottfredson and Hirschi 1990). For Gottfredson and Hirschi, criminal behavior provides quick and easy rewards with minimal effort. Those who commit crime, then, are likely to seek immediate gratification and have little ability or inclination to work toward long-term goals.

Gottfredson and Hirschi (1990) note that individual differences in the tendency to commit crime and deviance emerge early and are remarkably stable over the life course, with high-rate offenders remaining high-rate offenders when compared with others of the same age. The tendency to commit crime is also remarkably generalized, so that high-rate offenders are also more likely to engage in a variety of acts analogous to crime. These acts analogous to crime include accidents, illness, having or causing unwanted pregnancies, having unstable employment histories, and having unstable personal relationships. Avoiding accidents, maintaining relationships, and keeping a job all require caution, diligence, and hard work, traits that are weak among those with low self-control.

The offender for Gottfredson and Hirschi, then, is somewhat of a "loser." Offenders are not highly skilled, successful, smart, or hard-working. In addition, those with low self-control are not desirable as friends—they tend to be "unreliable, untrustworthy, selfish, and thoughtless" (1990: 157). This image of the typical offender is antithetical to the idea that crime is social behavior, motivated by a desire to conform to group norms. Self-control theory sees crime and deviance as "anti-group" behavior (Gottfredson and Hirschi 1990: 156) that "undermines harmonious group relations and the ability to achieve collective ends" (1990: 96). Further, Gottfredson and Hirschi explicitly deny that low self-control is the result of any sort of learning process or overt pressure to commit crime.

Clearly, then, the idea in learning theories that social reinforcement from one's friends or associates is an important cause of deviant behavior is contrary to Gottfredson and Hirschi's perspective. Self-control theorists have argued instead that the statistical association between deviant friends and deviant behavior is in part the result of self-selection and in part a statistical artifact created by the common practice of asking peers to report on each other's behavior (Gottfredson and Hirschi 1990). There is, in fact, substantial evidence that survey respondents assume greater behavioral similarly with their friends than actually exists, artificially inflating the association (Rebellon and Modecki 2014). However, the peer–delinquency relationship remains when independent measures of peer delinquency are used and self-selection is taken into account (Haynie and Osgood 2005), suggesting the existence of a causal relationship between delinquency and peer delinquency that control theories have as yet been unable to explain.

There is a long line of research that pits social control theories against cultural explanations of crime. This is likely due to the clear points of disagreement between the two theories, and Hirschi's framing of his initial test of social control theory against hypotheses derived from cultural deviance and other theories. Although it is widely acknowledged that self-selection plays an important role in explaining the correlation between delinquent peers and delinquency, the existence of a remaining correlation is often taken as evidence that disproves control theory, even though Hirschi himself acknowledged that social control theory failed to account adequately for this correlation. As he put it, "The first difficulty [the theory] encountered was the companionship factor, the importance of which was underestimated in the initial statement of the theory and in the data collection instrument" (2002: 230). Hirschi held that this was probably due to his assumption of natural motivation to delinquency, which failed to adequately consider "what delinquency does for the adolescent," in the explanation of delinquency (2002: 230). He further predicted that, "when the processes through which these variables [including peer delinquency] affect delinquency are spelled out, they will supplement rather than seriously modify the control theory" (2002: 231).

It is interesting that more than 40 years after the publication of *Causes of Delinquency*, we are still largely in the dark about the processes or mechanisms through which delinquent peers influence delinquent behavior (Bruinsma 1992; Paternoster et al. 2012; Reed and Rose 1998; Warr 2002; Young and Weerman 2013). The lack of consideration of alternatives to socialization versus selection is probably due in part to the lively debates between proponents of these two perspectives, and an empirical approach that focused too heavily on new methods of statistical analysis and not enough on improving the quality of the data being analyzed. The most sophisticated statistical methods cannot overcome the problem of not asking our respondents the right questions.

In any case, the lack of adequate attention to the mechanisms of peer influence has led to a premature conclusion that control theory cannot account for the correlation between peer delinquency and delinquency that remains after controlling for self-selection effects and methodological artifacts inflating the correlation. Much, if not most, research on this relationship has simply assumed that evidence of a causal relationship between peer delinquency and the individual's delinquency is automatically evidence in favor of a socialization effect consistent with cultural deviance theories. This false dichotomy is evident in much literature that contrasts "selection and socialization" effects, as if those are the only two options. For example, Kandel's (1978) oft-cited article published in the *American Journal of Sociology* is titled, "Homophily, Selection, and Socialization in Adolescent Friendships," even though there are no measures of actual processes of socialization or learning in the analyses. In this study, if dissimilar friends became more similar after their friendship began, this was taken as evidence for a "socialization" effect, even though there were no measures of reinforcement for deviance or attitudes toward deviant behavior in the study.

There are numerous examples in the literature of researchers simply assuming that a causal relationship between friends' deviance and the individual's deviance is due to socialization or learning processes, in many cases where measures of norm transference, attitudes toward deviance, or reinforcement for deviance are not even included in the analyses or present in the data set (Costello 2010). For example, Matsueda and Anderson (1998) find greater support for self-selection than peer influence on behavior, but they conclude that the remaining variance is evidence of a causal relationship between peers and behavior and is "contrary to control theories and consistent with learning theories" (1998: 299). There were no measures of attitudes toward deviance in their analysis, thus precluding a true test of learning theory. Similarly, Haynie (2001) found that members of cohesive delinquent peer networks have higher levels of delinquency, and that members of cohesive non-delinquent peer networks have lower levels of delinquency. She concluded that these findings support control theory, but that they are "even more compatible with differential association and social learning theories' emphasis on the importance of the context of friendship networks" (2001: 1049). There were no measures of the learning process or attitudes toward deviance in her analysis. McGloin's (2009) review of the literature on delinquent peers concludes that there is "an impressive stack of empirical literature" that supports the socialization perspective, even though she acknowledges that most tests of that perspective measure mere exposure to delinquent peers rather than the actual learning process.

Part of the reason for the assumption that a causal effect of delinquent friends on delinquency is supportive of cultural deviance or learning theories is no doubt the lack of research into alternative causal mechanisms, and even a lack of appropriate terminology with which to discuss alternative mechanisms. One example of this is found in Warr's (2002) book dedicated to the issue of the peer delinquency/delinquency connection. Throughout the book, Warr cites his own and others' research that casts doubt on the ability of learning or norm transference to explain the peer effect. For example, Warr and Stafford (1991) found that the effect of deviant peers on the individual's deviance was even stronger than the effect of the individual's own attitudes, suggesting that characteristics of the situation, rather than learned attitudes, explain the correlation. In the concluding chapter of his book, Warr states that "available evidence consistently fails to support the notion of attitude transference when it comes to peer influence and delinquency" (2002: 135). However, he also argues that "groups can develop their own moral codes, codes that offer moral legitimacy to the activities of the group" (2002: 70). Similar contradictions occur with Warr's use of the term peer pressure, a concept that he resoundingly rejects in the conclusion of his book, referring to peer pressure as an "everyday adage . . . suitable only for afternoons at the pub" (2002: 139). However, Warr also uses this term several times to explain peer influence. He states, "among adolescents with strong bonds to parents, the potential loss of parental approval . . . may be sufficient to deter delinquency even when pressure from peers is strong" (2002: 111), and quotes from one of his earlier works in which the terms "pressure of peers" and "peer-induced pressures" are used (2002: 113). Without more research on exactly *how* peers can cause changes in each other's behavior, it is perhaps inevitable that such terms continue to appear in the literature even when authors' intended meaning is not well-reflected by those terms.

In sum, much of the theoretical work in sociology dealing with the peer delinquency/delinquency relationship is couched in terms that pit self-selection and control theories against a cause and effect relationship and cultural deviance or learning theories. This false dichotomy has led many researchers to neglect other possible causal mechanisms that are or may be consistent with control theories, notably a simple opportunity effect (Felson 2003; Osgood and Anderson 2004; Warr 2002). This and other alternative explanations for the peer delinquency/delinquency relationship will be explored in more detail below. First, however, the empirical literature on the peer effect is discussed in more detail.

Research on the Peer Delinquency/Delinquency Relationship

There are a number of different themes in the existing literature on the peer–delinquency relationship. We start by reviewing the earliest literature on this connection, and discuss how methodological advances influenced the direction and focus of research. We then move to a discussion of the psychological literature on children's friendships, which has some similarities to the criminological literature on the role of friends, but which has focused more on friends as a positive influence. Finally, we review the literature in criminology on the relationship between attachment to friends and delinquency, which has important theoretical implications for the control theory/learning theory debate.

Methodological Approaches to the Peer–Delinquency Relationship

The empirical fact that delinquent behavior often occurs in groups, and the fact that delinquents tend to have delinquent friends, has been observed for centuries. As Warr (2002) notes in his review of the literature, early sociological studies such as those of Shaw and McKay (1942) focused on the robust patterns of group offending among youth that were evident in official reports of crime. With the development of self-report methodology, researchers continued to find evidence of this pattern (Warr 2002). Self-report methods also made it even easier to detect both group offending and the characteristics of offenders' friends, relationships with family, and offenders' attitudes toward crime (e.g. Hirschi 1969; Reiss and Rhodes 1964).

The earliest studies of peer delinquency simply asked youths to report on their associations with "juvenile delinquents" or "criminals," and merely provided correlational evidence demonstrating associations between deviant companions and deviant behavior (Erickson 1971; Short 1957). Later studies became more sophisticated both in terms of measurement and statistical techniques, including not only measures of delinquent associates, but also measures of attitudes toward crime and measures drawn from other theoretical explanations as controls. For example, Hirschi (1969) used a self-report study to measure his concept belief in the moral validity of the law, Sykes and Matza's (1957) techniques of neutralization, and measures of "focal concerns" thought to be characteristic of a lower-class culture (Miller 1958). The complexity of his analyses relative to the earliest studies of delinquent peers allowed him to conclude, for example, that there was virtually no evidence of a lower-class culture with their own focal concerns as Miller (1958) argued. Further, Hirschi concluded that:

> There is a very strong tendency for boys to have friends whose activities are congruent with their own attitudes. Boys with a large stake in conformity are unlikely to have delinquent friends, and even when a boy with a large stake in conformity does have delinquent friends, the chance that he will commit delinquent acts is relatively low.
>
> *(1969: 159)*

Similarly, Jensen's (1972) study using Hirschi's data allowed him to separate out the effects of delinquent associations, attitudes toward delinquency, and social bonds, and allowed him to conclude:

> Just as actual and potential reactions of delinquent peers can influence behavior without necessarily shaping normative commitments at the same time, so the sensitivity of children to the actual and potential reactions of their parents may shape their behavior even if they do not form commitments to such standards. The theory of differential association stresses "definitions" and "cultural" variables (values, norms, and beliefs) to such an extent that processes shaping human behavior other than internalization of normative standards tend to be slighted.
>
> *(1972: 574)*

Research continuing into the 1980s and 1990s similarly focused on statistical controls to tease out the relative impact and causal ordering of delinquent friends, social controls, attitudes toward crime, and delinquent behavior (Agnew 1993; Burkett and Jensen 1975; Johnson, Marcos, and Bahr 1987; Minor 1984), in some cases with increasingly sophisticated methodological tools designed to more precisely specify causal order and effect size between variables (Costello and Vowell 1999; Matsueda 1982). For the most part, however, studies on the delinquency/delinquent peer connection have utilized the same or similar measures that have been used since the earliest studies of the relationship, and it's far more common to see calls for increased attention to mechanisms of influence than it is to see analyses that allow examination of those mechanisms. For example, McGloin and Nguyen's (2012) study of instigation in delinquent groups notes that instigation toward deviant behavior might involve providing an idea or the motivation for crime, making a case for the likely success of the crime, pointing out opportunity for crime, or active pressure or coercion to commit a crime. However, as is the case with virtually all other such research, their data and methods do not allow an investigation into these possibilities.

A new methodological trend in the literature on the peer–delinquency connection is social network analysis. Originally referred to as "sociometry," this method of study can be traced back to the 1930s and the work of Jacob Moreno, who also founded the short-lived journal *Sociometry* (Freeman 2004). Network analysis has only recently become very popular in sociology, particularly from the mid-1990s and into the first decade of the new century (Wasserman, Scott, and Carrington 2005).

Social network analysis in its purest form does not attempt to explain individual behavior, but rather focuses on the structure of the group, and uses relations between members of the group as its fundamental unit of analysis (Wasserman and Faust 1994). Typically in criminological research, an individual's network measurements are treated as individual-level variables, a usage Wasserman and Faust refer to as "auxiliary network studies" (1994: 9). For example, this method allows the researcher to treat the density of an individual's peer group, or the extent to which each member of the group knows the other members, as a characteristic of that individual, i.e., as being a member of a more or less dense peer group. This type of analysis can also allow examination of balance or imbalance in friendship groups or dyads, and its effect on the behavior of group members over time (McGloin 2009). Haynie's (2001) study utilizing network analysis to understand the peer delinquency/delinquency relationship is one of the earliest and most frequently cited applications of network analysis to the explanation of delinquent behavior. In this study, Haynie finds that the correlation between delinquency and peer delinquency is conditioned by network characteristics, so for example denser peer networks show stronger delinquency/peer delinquency connections than less dense networks. While analyses like these can illuminate important characteristics of groups, they still cannot provide insight into the *mechanisms* that account for any causal effect of delinquent peers on delinquency. For example, Haynie argues that denser networks place more "constraint" on the behavior of their members toward delinquent or non-delinquent behavior (2001: 1048), and suggests that social networks "reinforc[e] social norms and beliefs" (2001: 1021). However, the variables used in her analysis do not measure social norms or reinforcement for adhering to group norms, so we cannot conclude that the delinquency/peer delinquency connection in these groups is a result of those mechanisms.

An increasing number of studies using network analysis methods have similarly uncovered important patterns related to group composition and offending, but like Haynie's, these studies typically don't include measures of the actual mechanism of influence. For example, Sarnecki's (2001) large-scale study of delinquent youth groups in Stockholm, Sweden, determined that co-offending groups are extremely short-lived and not densely linked, casting doubt on the idea that youths who are strongly tied to their friends are learning deviant norms and behavior from them. However, given the structural nature of Sarnecki's study, it isn't possible to definitively determine whether learning accounts for delinquency, because learning processes are not measured.

A number of studies focusing on gangs have also used network analytical techniques (e.g., Fleisher 2006; Roman et al. 2012), finding for example that individuals with different and separate groups of friends are less likely to be delinquent, and that less dense networks provide greater opportunities for successful delinquency reduction techniques (Roman et al. 2012). Like Sarnecki's (2001) study, however, these studies typically do not include measures of actual influence mechanisms.

Lonardo et al. (2009) conducted a sophisticated analysis of the effects on delinquency of enmeshment in deviant peer groups, having deviant romantic partners, and having deviant parents, and were able to conclude that having deviant romantic partners has an important effect on the individual's level of deviance even when friends' and parents' behavior is controlled. They hold that social networks "exert pressure" on the individual to conform to the group, and "constrain the behaviors" of their members (2009: 368), but again, no measures of pressure or other forms of group influence are included in the analyses. Haynie et al. (2005) similarly find that romantic partners can affect youths' behavior, but they note that their study cannot reveal the mechanisms underlying the network effects they document.

Recent studies analyzing network effects on cigarette smoking have been designed to tease out selection effects versus actual influence of friends' smoking (Mercken et al. 2010), and the effect of network centrality, density, and embeddedness on smoking behavior (Ennett et al. 2006), but these studies are focused only on statistical evidence for group effects and again, they cannot examine the actual mechanisms of peer influence.

Recently developed, more sophisticated methods of conducting network analysis are also limited by the nature of network data. Weerman (2011) used a newly created tool known as SIENA to model selection and peer influence effects in a longitudinal study, and found a modest peer effect on delinquency such that some youths were likely to change their behavior to more closely match that of their schoolmates, controlling for other relevant factors. He is still unable, however, to explain how/why peers were likely to change their behavior in this regard, and notes that his research "should be perceived as one of the first steps in getting a more contextualized insight into the role of delinquent peers during adolescence" (2011: 281).

In sum, network analysis has shed light on a number of important issues regarding peer influence. It cannot, however, reveal much about how peer influence takes place, largely because this research has used the same or similar data sets used in previous research. Having data on specific network connections is beneficial, and it's especially beneficial to have data on peer delinquency using reports from the peers themselves rather than estimates from their friends, as in the often-used Add Health data. However, we need to go beyond looking for correlations between individuals' and their friends' attitudes and behavior to uncovering the mechanisms of peer influence. In sum, existing social network analyses cannot answer the basic questions that are the focus of this research—how and why do friends have an influence on each other's behavior?

Literature on Children's Friendships

Most of the research on children's friendships has been conducted by psychologists and educational psychologists, and tends to take a broader view on peer influence than the literature in criminology. Because this literature is looking at a broad range of behavioral and psychological outcomes, it focuses on both positive and negative effects of friendships among children and adolescents.

Much of the psychological literature emphasizes the benefits of friendships for children, especially younger children, and discusses the positive effects of having friends on children's "adjustment" or "competence," as measured by variables such as academic achievement and prosocial behavior. In much of this literature, it seems taken for granted that having good relationships with friends is associated with less negative or delinquent behavior. For example, Wentzel, Donlan, and Morrison (2012) argue that adolescents with positive relationships with peers have higher levels of "emotional well-being," more positive "beliefs about the self," and display stronger "values for prosocial forms of behavior" than youths with less positive relationships with peers (2012: 79). Some research shows that children who are rated as sociometrically popular, or widely accepted by peers, are also rated by peers as being kind, trustworthy, and cooperative (Cillessen and Mayeux 2004). Barry and Wentzel (2006) found that adolescents with friends were more likely to be prosocial than those without friends, and that friends can act as agents of socialization to produce prosocial behavior. Research shows that friends encourage socially desirable behavior in one another (Berndt and Murphy 2002) and that children can have positive effects on each other's behavior in school (Berndt and Keefe 1995). There is also evidence that children can positively influence each other's academic performance (Epstein 1983) and academic achievement motivation (Nelson and DeBacker 2008). Bukowski, Newcomb, and Hartup go so far as to say, "No one has ever reported that having friends is correlated with undesirable social attributes" (1996: 5).

This focus on the positive effects of friends is one clear difference between the sociological and psychological literature, but there are also similarities. In general, peer similarity on a number of characteristics is noted in the psychological literature as well as the criminological literature (Brechwald and Prinstein 2011; Brown and Klute 2003; Ennett and Bauman 1994; Hamm, Hoffman, and Farmer 2012; Hartup 1992). Similar to longitudinal studies in criminology, longitudinal studies conducted by psychologists also find increased behavioral similarity between friends over time. For example, Wentzel, Barry, and Caldwell (2004) followed middle school students for two years and found that friends' prosocial behavior in 6th grade was correlated with the individual's prosocial behavior in 8th grade, showing both improvements in behavior for those initially lower than their friends in prosocial behavior and decreases in prosocial behavior for those initially higher. Andrews et al. (2002) found that peer binge drinking and cigarette smoking predicted the individual's subsequent engagement in those behaviors as young adults.

As noted above with regard to the criminological literature, there is often an assumption in the psychological literature that evidence of similarity in behavior is supportive of a social learning explanation, even when measures of the learning process are not included in the analysis (see, e.g., Allen and Antonishak 2008; Andrews et al. 2002; Barry and Wentzel 2006; Furman and Simon 2008; Hamm, Hoffman, and Farmer 2012; Prentice 2008; Ryan 2000; Wentzel, Barry, and Caldwell 2004). As some scholars in the field have noted (Jaccard, Blanton, and Dodge 2005), it is not safe to conclude that an apparent peer effect on behavior is genuine, and most psychological studies do not attempt to control for other relevant variables that could explain peer similarity.

Another similarity between the psychological and criminological literatures is the frequently mentioned lack of clear understanding of the many possible mechanisms of peer influence. Some examples of lists of possible mechanisms of influence include:

- Modeling, reinforcement, information exchange, expectancy socialization, emotional support (Altermatt 2012).
- Reinforcement for deviant talk, or "deviancy training" (Dishion et al. 1996).
- Peer pressure, behavioral display, antagonistic behaviors such as ridicule, threatening, or bullying, behavioral reinforcement, structuring of opportunities (Brown et al. 2008).
- Experience of "parallel events" (Jaccard, Blanton, and Dodge 2005) or a shared environment (Jussim and Osgood 1989), both of which refer to the possibility that friends' behavior becomes more similar over time because they're sharing important internal (developmental) or external conditions.
- Modeling, social reward and punishment, vicarious reinforcement and observational learning, and emulation of others' behavior to develop a positive identity or favorable sense of self (Brechwald and Prinstein 2011).
- Feelings of inadequacy or shame for nonconformity with a group, avoidance of social isolation, and avoidance of ridicule (Lashbrook 2000).

As with the criminological literature, there are more suggestions and possibilities in the psychological literature than there are actual studies that can shed light on these possible mechanisms. Evidence that there is increased similarity in peers' behavior over time is not sufficient to tease out those mechanisms (Gifford-Smith et al. 2005), and we are still left with more questions than answers.

The Issue of Attachment to Friends

It is interesting that the psychological literature on children's friendships is not more frequently cited in the criminological literature, particularly given that there has been a great deal of attention in criminology to the relationship between attachment to friends and delinquency. Similar to the literature on self-selection versus socialization, most of this literature pits control theories against learning or cultural deviance theories. Consistent with both common sense and Sutherland's differential association theory, we would expect that behavior and norms that are socially learned are more likely to be learned from others with whom we have stronger ties. As noted earlier, differential association and differential association-reinforcement theory hold that we are more likely to learn "definitions" from those with whom we have closer, more "intense" relationships (Akers 1998; Sutherland, Cressey, and Luckenbill 1992: 89).

Hirschi (1969) directly challenged the conception of delinquent companions as having very strong bonds with each other. Hirschi was reacting in part to views such as those of Albert Cohen, who stated that "relations with gang members tend to be intensely solidary and imperious" (1955: 31, cited in Hirschi 1969: 139) and that "the gang is a separate, distinct and often irresistible focus of attraction, loyalty, and solidarity (1955: 31). Views similar to Cohen's were noted by Sherif, Sherif, and Murphy (1964: 66), who held that "those personal characteristics ordinarily prized in social life—friendliness, sociability, loyalty—[are] associated with longer and more serious participation in activities labeled 'antisocial'" (cited in Hirschi 1969: 139). In contrast to these views, Hirschi argued that those with weak social bonds in one respect, such as attachment to parents or the school, would be unlikely to have strong bonds in other respects. Rather, citing Yablonsky's study of gang members, he held that the most delinquent youth come from "a social milieu that trains [the delinquent youth] inadequately for assuming constructive social roles" and fails to teach "human feelings of compassion or responsibility for another" (Yablonsky 1963: 196, cited in Hirschi 1969: 141). Consistent with Yablonksy's views, Hirschi stated that "It seems reasonable to conclude that persons whose social relations are cold and brittle, whose social skills are severely limited, are incapable of influencing each other in the manner suggested by those who see the peer group as the decisive factor in delinquency" (1969: 141).

The phrase "cold and brittle" is one that has been repeated often in the literature, and we argue that it has been overemphasized and at times used out of the context of Hirschi's disagreement with the notion that relationships among delinquent youth are "unusually warm" and that "delinquents are unusually dependent upon their peers" and "unusually likely to sacrifice [his] personal advantage to the 'requirements of the group'" (1969: 145). For example, a recent study of the relationship between delinquency and quality of adolescents' romantic relationships is titled, "Hirschi's 'Cold and Brittle' Hypothesis" (Giordano et al. 2010: 919), and that phrase has been repeated in some of the most frequently cited studies of the relationship between friendships and delinquency (e.g., Giordano, Cernkovich, and Pugh 1986: 1170; Kandel and Davies 1991: 442). The overemphasis on that phrase seems to imply that anyone who has engaged in any delinquent acts will have no close friendships, which clearly misrepresents Hirschi's hypothesis, particularly when we consider how common the more minor delinquent acts are in the population—50% of high school seniors in 2011 reported ever using one or more illicit drug, for example (Johnston et al. 2012; see also Elliott, Huizinga, and Menard 1989).

In any case, Hirschi clearly hypothesized that attachment to friends is negatively associated with delinquency. To assess the relationship between attachment to friends and delinquency, Hirschi first examined the relationship between attachment to friends and other elements of the social bond. Hirschi found that youths who were attached to their parents and who were committed to education were more likely to be attached to their peers as well (Hirschi 1969). Hirschi concluded from these findings that a high level of attachment to peers is not likely to produce the kinds of attitudes that tend to increase the likelihood of delinquency, in that both attachment to parents and achievement motivation are negatively associated with delinquency.

The direct relationship between attachment to peers and delinquency was assessed using measures of affectional identification with friends (measured with the question "Would you like to be the kind of person your best friends are?"), respect for best friends' opinions about important matters, and two measures of delinquency (Hirschi 1969: 258). These tests again supported the predictions of the theory, in that boys with stronger bonds to their friends were less likely to have self-reported delinquent acts and were less likely to perceive themselves as delinquent. Further, strong peer attachment (even to delinquent friends) seemed to reduce the individual's level of delinquency. This finding was at odds with differential association theory, which predicts that the effect of delinquent friends on the individual's delinquency will be stronger when the individual's level of attachment to them is higher.

Hirschi conducted further analyses to assess the relative merits of social control and differential association theories. The two key findings to emerge from these analyses were: 1) boys with stronger social bonds were less likely to have delinquent friends, and 2) the stronger the stake in conformity, the weaker the correlation between delinquent friends and delinquency. Thus, despite the finding that having more delinquent friends was correlated with higher levels of delinquency, Hirschi found that the strength of other social bonds reduced both the likelihood of having delinquent friends and the relationship between delinquent friends and delinquency. He concluded from these findings that the likelihood of having delinquent friends is largely dependent on a self-selection process, where similar boys who are already likely to engage in delinquency come together as friends, rather than friends having a "bad influence" on one another.

Hirschi's findings of a negative relationship between attachment to peers and delinquency have not been confirmed in many other studies, however. Although some studies have found a negative relationship between attachment to friends and delinquency (Rosenbaum 1987; Sampson and Laub 1993), others have found the opposite, that attachment to friends is weakly but positively related to delinquent behavior (Alarid, Burton, and Cullen 2000; Gardner and Shoemaker 1989; Heimer 1996; Hindelang 1973). Other studies find that attachment to friends and delinquency are not significantly correlated (Krohn and Massey 1980; Vasquez and Zimmerman 2014; Wiatrowski, Griswold, and Roberts 1981). In studies focusing on friendships among delinquents and non-delinquents, Giordano, Cernkovich, and Pugh (1986) and Kandel and Davies (1991) both found little difference between them. It is important to note, however, that measures of attachment vary in quality. Some studies use the amount of time an individual spends with friends as the single measure of attachment to friends. This operationalization of attachment to friends was criticized by Hirschi in *Causes of Delinquency* (Hirschi 1969: 160), and could just as easily be used as a measure of opportunity for deviance (Osgood and Anderson 2004). In addition, many studies explicitly focusing on the role of peers in producing delinquency exclude measures of attachment to peers, and obviously cannot inform the debate on this issue (Jensen 1972; Johnson, Marcos, and Bahr 1987; Matsueda and Anderson 1998; Patterson and Dishion 1985; Thornberry et al. 1994; Warr 1993).

The peer–delinquency research in psychology shows similar ambiguity in the relationship between attachment to friends and deviance (Gifford-Smith et al. 2005). For example, Andrews et al. (2002) found increased peer influence on marijuana use among those with better quality relationships with same-sex peers for women but not for men. The same study found increased peer influence on marijuana use among men with better quality relationships with opposite-sex peers, but not among women. It is difficult to make any general statements about the relationship given the inconsistency in these findings.

Another line of research in psychology that is relevant to this issue focuses on peer rejection. A number of studies show that aggressive or antisocial children tend to be rejected by peers, and then tend to form friendships with similarly rejected peers and go on to engage in further deviant behavior (Dishion and Patterson 2006; Dishion, Piehler, and Myers 2008). Experimental research has demonstrated that previously unacquainted children who engage in aggressive behavior are likely to be rejected by their peers (Coie and Kupersmidt 1983; Dodge 1983), and that aggressive children are commonly disliked (Hartup 1992). A number of studies of children's popularity among peers show that aggressive children are less likely to be rated by their peers as "popular" (Wentzel and Asher 1995; Wentzel, Donlan, and Morrison 2012). These models suggest that although more deviant children might have friendships, they are formed as a result of rejection from the wider peer group, which is consistent with the idea that deviant youths are less successful socially. This image of young offenders is more consistent with Hirschi's (1969) claims about the nature of social relationships among delinquent youth than it is with much of the research in criminology showing little difference in friendships between delinquents and non-delinquents. As Chapple (2005) notes, this pattern is also consistent with Gottfredson and Hirschi's claim that low self-control leads to a wide range of negative behaviors and consequences, including poor social relationships and deviant behavior.

Clearly, the relationship between attachment to peers and delinquency has remained contentious. However, we argue that the evidence on this issue has been used unfairly to discount the claims of control theory when in fact the research showing little relationship between attachment to friends and delinquency is at least as damaging to learning or cultural deviance theories as it is to control theories. This has been acknowledged in the literature at times—for example, when Giordano, Cernkovich, and Pugh (1986: 1170) note that both "cold and brittle" and "intimate fraternity" images of delinquent friendships are oversimplified.

The Current Research

In the chapters that follow, we provide insight into three understudied questions. 1) To the extent that friends do have a causal influence in producing deviant behavior in one another, exactly how does that happen? Which of the many noted possible mechanisms of peer influence, such as overt pressure, ridicule, teaching norms conducive to deviance, providing opportunity for deviance, etc. are actually in effect, and what mechanisms are more or less common? 2) How common are attempts at positive influence, and what are the mechanisms by which peers influence each other toward non-deviant or prosocial behavior? 3) Are those with stronger bonds to friends, stronger social bonds overall, and higher levels of self-control more likely to try to influence their friends toward conformity, as control theories would predict? What factors determine the success or failure of influence attempts? The research we describe in the following chapters begins to uncover the answers to these important questions.

Note

1. According to Kandel (1978), this term was coined by Lazarsfeld and Merton (1954) and originally simply described the fact that friends tend to be similar to each other on a variety of characteristics, without explaining that fact. Warr and others use the term as synonymous to self-selection, or the idea that "people make friends with people who are similar to themselves" (2002: 41). Thus, in Kandel's use of the term, self-selection can explain homophily, but in Warr's use, self-selection is another term for homophily.

3

QUALITATIVE ACCOUNTS OF NEGATIVE PEER INFLUENCE

Although we know from prior research that a great deal of the "peer effect" is the result of self-selection, approximately half of the relationship between deviance and peer deviance remains unexplained. Possible mechanisms of influence that have been discussed in the literature range from the mundane, including a simple opportunity effect in which peers present each other with invitations to deviance that are readily accepted (Costello 1997; Felson 2003; McGloin and Nguyen 2012; Osgood and Anderson 2004) to the dramatic, in which peers ridicule each other for failure to deviate, pressure each other to deviate, or threaten to ostracize those who fail to deviate (Brown et al. 2008; Warr 2002). Because most studies of peer influence do not ask respondents to report on processes of group interaction, however, we simply have no information on how or why peers influence each other toward deviance. The analyses reported in this chapter are thus a first step in the process of uncovering the mechanisms by which peers influence each other's behavior toward deviance.

The data in this chapter are drawn from two sources. First, detailed accounts of incidents of peer influence were drawn from 81 papers written by students in an introductory sociology course at the University of Rhode Island (URI) in the Fall 2009 semester. The vast majority of students were first-year students. Students were given the opportunity to write papers for extra credit that described in detail incidents they directly witnessed or participated in that involved positive or negative peer influence. Papers were submitted anonymously, and credit was awarded based only on students' signed consent forms, which were submitted at the same time but separate from the papers. Students were also instructed to use pseudonyms for themselves and others to maintain their anonymity. (See Appendix A for the full instructions for the assignment.) Papers averaged two pages, typically about one page describing an incident of negative influence and one page describing an incident of positive influence. Students were especially encouraged to write about incidents of positive influence, as we expected those to be more difficult to recall.

Of the 81 papers submitted, there were 55 descriptions of negative influence and 74 descriptions of positive influence that met our criteria for inclusion in the study. Some of the papers didn't quite fit the guidelines provided for the assignment and were therefore not included in the analysis.

Instructions asked students to describe specific incidents, and some papers were excluded because the situations described were not specific enough. For example, respondent number 55 explained that a friend of hers had started skipping school and doing drugs after she starting dating a new boyfriend. This level of detail was insufficient to determine how or why the girl began engaging in deviant behavior, and was therefore not included in our analysis. Respondent number 52 described a situation of positive influence in which he and a group of friends tried to help a friend get over the trauma of his girlfriend breaking up with him. Because we are interested in peer influence on behavior rather than someone's psychological state, this paper was also excluded from our analysis. Because some papers described multiple incidents or some incidents were classified into more than one category, the number of coded incidents was 68 for negative-influence incidents and 89 for positive-influence incidents.[1]

The second source of qualitative data was student responses to two open-ended questions on our survey of 108 URI students and 723 University of Oklahoma (OU) students conducted in Spring semester 2012 (the complete surveys are described in Chapter 5). These questions asked students to describe an incident that they directly witnessed or participated in that involved positive peer influence and one that involved negative influence (see Appendix B for question wording). Most of the respondents answered the open-ended questions. Students at Oklahoma, who completed the survey online, gave much more detailed accounts than the URI students, who completed the survey in class on paper. Typical responses from URI students included,

> Stopping someone from drinking more at a party.

> Preventing a fight.

> I saw a friend of mine who doesn't normally drink coerced into doing so.

In contrast, Oklahoma students tended to write more detailed answers, such as:

> Recently I was at a party and a girl claimed to have seen a guy taking her licence[2] plate. I went looking for the guy and finding him, I got into a fight with him. I broke his jaw and he broke my nose. I regret it now, but we did recover the licence plate.

> I was volunteering at an event and had to work a 12–6 pm shift, and wasn't supposed to leave the event. An acquaintance of mine, "Nicole," tried to encourage me to sneak out and leave the event for a little while with her. Ultimately, she was not successful, as I chose to stay.

Overall, though, the richest source of qualitative data was the URI students' papers written for extra credit. Not surprisingly, they were much more detailed, and were more likely to include information on the thoughts of the students involved.[3] This provided more useful data for categorizing types of influence by the motives of those involved and the methods they used to influence their peers. For example, in the students' survey responses, it was very common for them to write things like:

> My girlfriend was pressured into drinking more than she should have on her birthday.

Comments like this were more difficult to code into detailed categories given the lack of information on how this "pressure" occurred, such as what was said or done, and the lack of information about why her companions would have engaged in such pressure. In comparison, comments like this one, from a student's paper, provide much more detail and context.

> . . . someone at a party was being pressured into drinking when they were abstaining from alcohol. One person was ridiculing the person for not wanting to drink at a party, and once word went around that this person did not want to drink, the negative influences came into play. A chant began, and soon the crowd at the party was negatively influenced by a small group of three or so, and this created a domino effect of chanting . . . I began to notice that people, who were known as 'good people' began getting involved in the chant as well . . .

Because the narratives in the student papers collected in 2009 were so much more detailed, we used those as a starting point for developing coding categories. These papers were read several times, first to get a general sense of common themes or patterns that seemed to appear. During the second reading we noted brief descriptions of the events described by the participants, and we then developed coding categories of these descriptions based in part on mechanisms of influence suggested in prior research (especially Warr 2002). The papers were then read a third time with an eye toward revealing any patterns that did not seem to fit our existing coding categories.

Our next step was to read and code the responses to the open-ended questions from the 2012 survey of Oklahoma and Rhode Island students. In our reading of these comments, we did not uncover any notable departures from the categories we created based on the 2009 student papers. Because the URI responses to the open-ended survey questions seemed to be less detailed than the Oklahoma responses, we first analyzed the two sets of responses separately to see if there were any differences in the patterns of responses. For the descriptions of negative influence attempts, the only difference in the patterns of responses between the URI and Oklahoma samples was that URI students reported more coercive influence attempts and the Oklahoma sample reported more simple offers or opportunity effects. This difference may be a reflection of possible regional differences in word choice, or it might reflect actual differences in the students' behavior. In either case, given the purposes of our research, we did not feel that this difference warranted separate analysis of the two sets of qualitative data.

Most of the comments written for the 2012 surveys were classified as "general pressure or influence" attempts, because they indicated some peer influence process but did not provide enough detail to classify them further. Students very commonly used phrases like "peer pressure," being "talked into" doing something, "encouraging" someone to do something, "argued" with someone about a behavior, "warned" someone against doing something, or "reprimanded" someone for doing something. Responses were put into this category when there was no additional information provided that would allow us to code them into another more specific category. However, as noted above, the student papers written in 2009 contained much more detailed accounts of incidents, and comparative analysis of the results of our coding the data into categories revealed this as well. Specifically, for negative influence attempts, the 2012 survey had a total of 422 usable student comments for both the Oklahoma and Rhode Island samples, but 269 of those (64%) were too general to classify beyond "general pressure or influence." In comparison, the 2009 papers had 69 usable accounts of negative peer influence, and only 12 (17%) were too general to classify beyond general pressure or influence. The numbers and percentages of negative influence attempts are presented in Table 3.1. Percentages for the more specific types of influence attempts are calculated after the "general pressure or influence" category was excluded. Detailed descriptions and examples of each type of influence are provided below.

TABLE 3.1 Negative influence mechanisms, Oklahoma and Rhode Island 2012 samples and Rhode Island 2009 sample

Influence Type	2012 Sample		2009 Sample	
	N	Percent★	N	Percent★
General pressure/influence	269	64%	12	17%
Emulation of admired models	11	8%	10	18%
Simple offer or invitation	63	48%	6	10%
Minimizing potential consequences	16	12%	12	21%
Coercive tactics	27	20%	17	30%
Entertainment of onlookers	22	17%	2	4%
Deviance loves company	4	3%	1	2%
Fear of loss of status	3	2%	4	7%
Other	4	3%	5	16%
N's	422		69	
N's excluding general pressure	132		57	

★ Percentages for categories other than general pressure or influence are calculated excluding general pressure or influence

Negative Influence Mechanisms

As noted previously, most of the descriptions of peer influence were very general and were classified as "general pressure or influence." Examples of these types of responses include:

> I was in the car with "Joe" and he started to go down a one way street before he realized he was going the wrong way. He wanted to turn around, but everyone else in the car, including me, convinced him to keep going, and Joe ended up getting pulled over.

> My roommate and I often convince each other to not attend classes.

> Friends of mine encouraged me to play drinking games even though I had to work the next day.

> My friends were trying to get me to do LSD the night before a big exam.

> Jenny kept calling me every night that week asking me if I was in or out [of a plan to drink alcohol in the bathroom at a sweet sixteen party.]

In these cases, it appeared that there was something more than a simple invitation to participate in a behavior, but there was not enough information provided to classify these responses into one or more of the more specific categories described below. Thus, these responses were not very helpful in understanding exactly how peer influence attempts are engaged in or what the motivation of the influencer was. However, the nature of most of these accounts clearly indicates that peers very frequently try to get each other to engage in deviant behavior when the individual may not be readily willing. Note that in three of the four examples above, the respondent hints at a potential negative consequence of the behavior ("the night before a big exam") or indicates reluctance to engage in the behavior. These accounts contradict much of what has been written about "peer pressure" in the literature, in that peer pressure is not thought to be a major cause of peer influence or the peer effect (Warr 2002). While our results do not show that non-deviant youths are being corrupted by deviant youths in any general way that could account for the delinquency/peer delinquency connection, they do show that situational peer pressure is common. In other words, these accounts demonstrate how having deviant friends could increase the frequency with which individuals engage in deviant behavior, if not explain the initiation into deviance.

Emulation of Admired Models

There were several types of peer influence described by our respondents that were similar to the accounts classified as general pressure or influence but were detailed enough for them to be distinguished as separate categories. The first of these we refer to as "emulation of admired models," and this was particularly common among the URI 2009 sample with 18% of respondents describing this process. In these cases, students report engaging in a deviant behavior that other, admired youths are engaging in, but without any mention of being pressured to engage in the behavior. For example, one respondent from the 2009 sample wrote:

> When I was fourteen, I hung out with my brother, my friend, and my friend's brother. Both my brother and my friend's brother could drive, so we spent most of our time riding around in their cars. One day we were parked at a bridge on our road and both of the brothers pulled out a pack of cigarettes and began to smoke them. My friend and I both looked up to our brothers and thought they were the best thing since sliced bread, so we asked if we could have one to share. When we smoked our first cigarette we got really light headed and liked it. So, we started smoking them to get light headed . . .

This respondent went on to describe a similar process that led to their initiation of marijuana use, and added that, "We spent most of our time and money smoking and buying pot just to get high with our brothers to be cool in their eyes."

This account is similar to many students' accounts of imitating the behavior of older kids who were perceived as "cool," but without any discussion of the older kids encouraging this behavior, pressuring the younger kids, or even inviting them to participate in the behavior. This process appears to be similar to the "perceived norms" explanation of alcohol use among college students, which argues that students believe that drinking is more common and more normative than it actually is on college campuses (Baer, Stacy, and Larimer 1991). Some research shows that students' actual drinking behavior is influenced by mistaken beliefs about what is expected of them, such as one study that found that women who think that men want them to drink more are more likely to drink to excess (LaBrie et al. 2009). Warr (2002) notes several similar mechanisms of influence such as Jones's (1964) concept "ingratiation" and Matza's (1964) concept "shared misunderstanding." In both of these conceptions, individuals signal agreement with or acceptance of a group's apparent beliefs in an attempt to be liked or accepted by the group. Many of our respondents were very clear in their motivation to adopt the deviant behavior of those they admired, as in the previous example and in this one:

At first I was hesitant to hang out with my team because they were all older than me. Sometimes they would go out and do things but I would say I was busy. However, my sophomore year, I became more comfortable in knowing they liked me so I went out with them more. That same year the older girls started drinking when we hung out. I had never drank before and even though they never forced me to drink, I felt the need to do it because they were and I looked up to these older girls. I wanted them to think I was cool and I wanted them to like me more.

A similar account:

I wouldn't exactly say that my first time doing any of this was because of peer pressure. It was more of a pressure to fit in, to be able to brag about it at school. My first time doing anything was in a shed in my friend's back yard. We had gone to his house because the boy I liked was over. In order to impress the boy, I smoked weed and played some beer pong. All my life I had been a straight-edge. I never thought I would be smoking a joint or partying on a Saturday afternoon. When we left my friend's, I didn't know what to think of myself. In a way, I felt older. In another way, I felt disappointed in myself. I knew this wasn't something my parents would approve of. I also knew that it wasn't something I had approved of less than a year before.

This account is particularly interesting in its clear ambivalence about the acceptability of the behavior, in that the respondent was clearly not motivated by beliefs or values that made the behavior acceptable to her, but rather by her belief that it would impress someone she liked. It also fits with the idea of "false uniqueness/pluralistic ignorance" described by Miller and McFarland (1987), which refers to individuals rejecting deviant group values, but assuming that other members of the group accept them. The same moral ambivalence is exhibited in this account:

. . . Chris [the respondent's "much older" boyfriend] told me him and a few of the guys were gunna smoke some weed. I've never smoked before, nor have I even been around people smoking. I knew I always wondered about it, but I was scared that my parents would find out. I didn't wanna tell him I couldn't smoke because I was scared of what my parents were going to think. I didn't want Chris to think I was a loser. So, when he asked me if I wanted to smoke, I had no choice but to say yes. I knew what I was doing was wrong, but I felt like I needed to fit in. Mariel already said she was going to do it, and I didn't want to be the only one to say know [sic]. So I smoked weed for the first time that night. I actually enjoyed it . . .

As can be seen in Table 3.1, these types of accounts were about twice as common among the 2009 sample than the 2012 sample, perhaps because the 2009 sample were almost all first-semester freshmen at the time, and many had recent memories of their earlier initiation into alcohol or drug use, likely in high school. There were, however, similar accounts among the 2012 sample, this one from an Oklahoma student:

There is negative peer influence all over campus. In classes, in the dorms, on the South Oval people are always talking about the cool "parties" they go to and if you don't go to them and say that you sound like an idiot. Again, I've never really been in a situation where someone has pressured me or my friends to drink, so I've never witnessed it first hand, but I know that the pressure is everywhere coming from nearly everyone it feels like.

The example below again shows how older youths can influence younger ones through their actions even if that influence may not be intentional.

Gathering of friends from a prominent student organization—alcohol was made available by older members in attendance, younger members were told they did not have to drink, but the implication was that abstaining meant they were not mature enough to handle something so adult. Indirect pressure and a permissive circumstance led most younger members—all minors—to drink.

This respondent offered his own thoughts on how peer context can influence behavior:

I know a kid who won't cuss around just me, but as soon as he is with the other guys he does it to fit in.

As noted previously, there is a great deal of evidence in the literature on college student drinking suggesting that students overestimate how much other students drink and how acceptable drinking is to other students (Bourgeois and Bowen 2001; Martens et al. 2006; Neighbors et al. 2006; Turrisi et al. 2007). These perceived drinking norms are associated with higher levels of alcohol use (Perkins, Haines, and Rice 2005). Some research shows that overestimation of other forms of peer deviance is also common, and the effects of overestimation of peer deviance on self-reported delinquency were twice as strong as the effects of actual peer delinquency (Young and Weerman 2013).

These processes appear to be operating among some of our respondents, at least for the minor forms of deviant behavior that were common in our sample. For whatever reasons, drinking, drug use, and partying are seen as "cool" among the youths in our sample, and even in the absence of pressure or encouragement from friends, youths will engage in these behaviors in an effort to enhance their social status or likeability to others. This is consistent with past research, which suggests that delinquent youth are seen by their peers as more "fun" than conventional youth (Rebellon 2006; Riley 1987). To some extent, these types of behaviors can also be seen as "claims to adult status," as Hirschi (1969: 162–70) put it—so drinking, smoking, and even getting tattoos could be a marker of independence from adults and adult rules for behavior. This could also simply be a factor of the sociability of partying—kids who are partying are almost invariably doing so with groups of other youths, giving the impression of popularity among peers. In addition, quiet nights alone or at the movies with a friend or two are rarely fodder for bragging about in class the next day or for posting pictures on social media. This probably artificially inflates youths' estimates of how common drinking and drug use are.

A related concept that could help explain the "perceived norms" process is the fundamental attribution error. This error in reasoning occurs when observers attribute an individual's behavior to some enduring quality or characteristic of that person, such as their attitudes (Jones and Harris 1967). The tendency to assume that one's behavior is determined by one's attitudes or values might lead individuals to assume that peers who are drinking approve of drinking, and therefore would approve of others' drinking as well. Conversely, observers of others' behavior might assume that failure to engage in similar behavior might indicate to the models of that behavior one's disapproval of the behavior. If one were seeking the approval of those engaging in the behavior, then, they might feel pressured to engage in that behavior regardless of the true attitudes of the models of that behavior.

Simple Offers or Invitations

Another commonly mentioned mechanism of peer influence is a simple invitation to deviant behavior that is readily accepted by the individual in question. It has been frequently noted in the literature that peers can provide opportunities for each other to engage in various behaviors that they may not have thought about engaging in alone (Costello 1997; Felson 2003; Osgood and Anderson 2004; Warr 2002). When young people are engaged in unstructured socializing with friends, they're free to suggest a variety of deviant behaviors that may increase the likelihood or frequency of engaging in these behaviors. College students, especially those living on campus or with same-aged roommates, are in a segregated social environment often composed entirely of similar-aged youths who are free of adult supervision and free of many adult responsibilities. It is not surprising, then, that they often suggest behavior to each other that might not be the most productive for them.

Deviant behavior that resulted from simple offers or invitations was the most common specific category of peer influence in our 2012 sample with 48% of specific influence attempts classified as such. It was noted in just over 10% of the 2009 sample as well. Typical accounts from students include the following:

> I am staying at a friends place and all of his roommates and their friends, who I am also friends with were smoking weed and passed me the pipe so I smoked even though I had been previously ambivalent about it because I hadn't smoked in several months.

> Last night, I was going home from the bar to get some rest. My good work friend and her attractive friends came out of their car and invited me to party with them. I really needed sleep, but I decided to spend more of my night out late drinking. It was very enjoyable until the next morning. I was exhausted all day. Their exorbitant attractiveness motivated me to stay up past when I said I would.

> There were many times when guys from my hall would ask me if I wanted to drink with them. I am adamantly against drinking, so I always declined their offers.

> In high school my friends wanted to skip class a lot and it didn't take much for me to go along with it.

Note that unlike cases in which the student described "pressure" or "influence" or "persuasion," none of these accounts had any indication of pressure or attempts to persuade anyone to do something they did not want to do, even in the case of the respondent who was repeatedly offered to drink with his dorm mates. These types of responses were also differentiated from the "emulation of admired models" category by a lack of discussion of feeling a need to participate in the behavior in order to fit in or win the approval of peers.

Some students' responses demonstrated individual differences in reactions to invitations to deviant behavior, such as this one:

> One time I went with my friends to a house party after we went to a club. They were offered drugs and so was I, they accepted and I didn't.

The following response also demonstrates a variety of individuals' reactions to the same invitation to deviance. It is also interesting in that the student who wrote this account did not participate in the deviant activity but was involved in persuading "Amy" to go ahead and smoke marijuana.

> Kaitlyn, a roommate, offered weed to me and some of my friends who were relaxing in the living room. One of my friends, Rhonda, said yes and smoked without second thought. My friend Arthur and I both declined and stuck to it, but the last person, Amy, went back and forth, at first saying no, but then with the persuasion of all of us for her to just do it, she eventually smoked too.

Another account demonstrates the power of opportunity to override one's values or beliefs that an activity was wrong:

> Marcus didn't have the time or ability to complete a very important homework assignment for one of his classes at OU. Marcus told his friend Stu who was in the same class, and later that evening, Stu sent Marcus an unsolicited copy of his homework for Marcus to adapt and use as his own, saying it wasn't a big deal. Even though Marcus knew it would be cheating, having all the answers was just too tempting. Marcus ended up turning in a variation of the assignment and received full credit.

Finally, the opportunity to drink to excess often presented itself in the form of peers buying drinks for each other. This was mentioned frequently by our respondents, several times in the context of someone trying to drink 21 shots of alcohol on their twenty-first birthday. Two examples are illustrative:

> One of my good friends does not like to hit on girls unless he is drunk. One of his friends kept giving him drinks, but he ended up having way too much and got really sick. He ended up throwing up at the bar in front of everyone. I would say that influence of that idiot friend WAS successful.

> To celebrate one of my friends turning 21, we all went out to a bar. I was designated driver and I was with my brother and two mutual friends. Basically, one friend kept ordering drinks for the other, but I feel like the other was too intoxicated to realize how much he was drinking. So the friend ordering the drinks should have observed how drunk his friend was getting, but he was pretty drunk himself, so maybe I shouldn't hold it against him. Anyway, I drove all of us back to their apartment (they're roommates) and the one whose birthday we were celebrating could barely even make it up the stairs. He was ok, but he had way too much to drink.

These accounts demonstrate that even when peers clearly have a causal influence on each other's behavior, it is often much more trivial than is assumed in much of the literature on the peer effect. None of these accounts includes any description of friends trying to teach each other values or norms in support of deviant behavior as learning theories would hold, and none of them includes any explicit notion of pressure toward deviance. Thus, these accounts provide support for the notion that at least some of the peer effect is the result of peers providing each other with opportunities to engage in deviance that they otherwise would not have had or perceived.

Coercive Tactics

In contrast to the simple opportunity effects noted above, some students' responses indicated a number of different types of coercive attempts to get someone to engage in deviant or dangerous behavior. Altogether, 20% of the 2012 sample responses and 30% of the 2009 sample reported behavior that we classified as coercive. These descriptions were all more detailed than those classified as "general pressure or influence" and often included terms that were more overtly coercive, such as "made me," "forced me," or someone telling someone they "had to" do something. For example:

> My friend was already pretty drunk and my friends including myself made her drink more and she ended up throwing up.

> I saw a friend of mine who doesn't normally drink coerced into doing so.

We classified a number of subtypes of coercion when student responses were more detailed. These included tricks, bribes, ridicule, and coercive appeals to friends' loyalty. The most common subtype of coercive influence was ridicule, and this was especially frequent among the URI 2009 sample with 19% of all classified influence attempts (including the general influence category) being classified as "ridicule." One typical incident involved a group of high school kids trying to convince a friend to play beer pong. One of the influencers wrote:

> . . . By then my other friends caught on, and so they were also saying, "C/mon, Grace, just play. You won't get drunk. What are you 5 years old?" We even told her she may as well learn beer pong and how to drink now because in college she would look ridiculous to never have drank.

This quote also points out how multiple types of influence often overlapped, in this case, we see some effect of perceived college drinking norms and the minimization of potential consequences of behaviors (described later) when the group tells Grace she won't get drunk.

Many attempts at ridicule got at the idea that refusing to engage in a deviant behavior was immature or the respondent was a "baby," and a number of our respondents also reported ridicule in the form of insults to one's masculinity, as in this example:

> . . . Kyle's friends started to call Kyle some derogatory names since he wasn't drinking with the guys. Just because he wouldn't drink they called him "gay" and other names that in no way described him.

Similarly, one respondent described an incident in which he was driving on a divided highway and needed to turn around, and,

> . . . I was scared because not only was it illegal to make the U-turn, but also there were cars traveling 50 miles per hour. They kept yelling at me saying "You're such as pussy! You don't have any balls! Grow up and just turn here!"

Another example that touches on issues of proving one's masculinity is:

> . . . The guys would make fun of those who did not steal or be 'rebellious' like they were. Girls would even start stealing in order to catch the attention of a certain boy or show how 'cool' they were. The boys would severely make fun of the other boys who did not steal, girls who did not was not a big issue. They would harass other boys with words such as "pussy" or "fag" just to prove how tough they were.

Another incident provides a snapshot of fraternity life, and could also provide some insight into the quality of some of our students' writing:

> Last night I was trying to write an essay that was due this morning and several of my brothers busted into my room demanding I drink and smoke weed with them. I explained that alcohol would kill my addy [Adderall] buzz (even though I don't think it does and I wasn't even taking any at the time), and that I was trying to write an essay. They mostly understood (although repeatedly calling me a pussy) and agreed to leave if I chugged the rest of a Coors one had and shotgunned a Miller High Life tall boy with them. I agreed, but having not eaten yet that day (woke up at 6pm) I got a little light headed. It wore off soon enough and I finished my essay. I feel pretty good about it. Their attempt was semi- successful, but I'm glad we were able to come to a compromise.

The term "pussy" was used frequently by our respondents in describing incidents of ridicule:

> I encouraged my friend to not be a "pussy" and drink more since he was not driving.

> One roommate was giving the other a hard time about being so pussy whipped over a girl who had not slept with him yet. The razed roommate tried to shrug it off and joke that she would. After a few weeks of this teasing the razed roommate broke up with the girlfriend who he had wanted to marry. He had even gone to look at rings and had picked one out, but then decided that they were too different, and broke up.

The example below combines ridicule with a motivation to get someone to engage in deviance for the entertainment or amusement of peers (described in more detail below).

> A group of friends found out that one of my friends had never been drunk enough to puke, so we tried to get him that drunk by mocking him for not being able to drink enough, etc. We called him names and pressured him until he was very drunk, but he didn't actually throw up.

As Warr (2002) notes, research on ridicule among youth groups reveals that it is both common and a potentially powerful form of group influence toward deviance. Ridicule signals possible rejection by peers, which might have a powerful effect on behavior, particularly for adolescents and young adults. Lashbrook (2000) argues that ridicule or the threat of expulsion from a group can lead to emotional reactions such as feelings of shame, which in turn can serve as motivating forces leading to conformity to a group. In his analysis of interview data with a small sample of college students, Lashbrook (2000) found that isolation or fear of ostracism from a group and the experience of ridicule or fear of ridicule were frequently mentioned as important determinants of college students' participation in drinking or drug use. The question of why peers are sometimes motivated to exert pressure on their peers to drink or engage in other forms of deviance is another issue, however, which we address below.

Some other examples of coercion that were less common in our data on negative influence included the use of tricks, bribes, or coercive appeals to loyalty. Examples of each follow.

Tricks

James T. Kirk gave Spock a drink without informing him of its contents.

Carly had brought a flask with her to restaurant late at night. She encouraged Leslie and Max to drink with her by masking the alcohol by mixing it with a drink from the restaurant.

Bribes

"Lucy" would tell the girls that they could spend the night at her house if they joined in on bullying one certain girl. Of course at the age of 13 all we wanted was to be Lucy's "best friend" and did whatever Lucy told us to do. It was almost as if she was the ringleader of all the girls in the 8th grade class.

Coercive Appeals to Loyalty

I was at a party recently and I didn't want to drink anymore but my friend just wanted to "finish the bottle" and made me feel guilty for not wanting to take more shots than I was comfortable with in such a short amount of time.

. . . Edward is really good at getting people to do what he wants by making them feel guilty. Edward also tried to make me feel guilty by saying things like "I wish my best friend could trip with me . . ." when I disapprove of their activities.

Minimizing Potential Consequences of Deviance

Another common method of negative peer influence among our respondents was to try to convince someone to engage in deviant behavior by claiming that the potential consequences were negligible or benign. This technique was more common in the 2009 URI sample with 21% of specific influence attempts falling into this category, compared to 12% in the 2012 sample. There were two common subtypes of this method, the first minimizing health or safety-related consequences of a behavior. For example, one friend tried to convince another to try smoking marijuana for the first time by claiming that "It's proven to be more healthy for you than cigarettes and plus it's all natural no chemicals or anything." This and a similar circumstance resulted in the reluctant person giving in and smoking:

. . . They could tell I was uncomfortable so they were like well do you want to? I was just like umm I don't know. Michelle was like "well what else are we going to do? There's nothing ever to do here!" That just made it more awkward because if I was the only one who didn't want to then what were we going to do for the rest of the night. They were all like "come on like its not even bad you won't even get high the first time I guarantee." Mark was like "seriously what are you scared about nothing bad is going to happen to you we do this everyday and we know what we're doing."

Another example is drawn from an account of an evening where the driver had become too drunk to drive the group home, two members of which had never driven a car before. Despite the fact that it was snowing, someone suggested that one of the two friends who had never driven should drive the group home. The student writes:

> In response to this everyone was sitting there explaining how easy it would be to drive. The way home was all back roads and we would be able to go as slow as possible because no one would be on the roads . . . she assured me she would be ok as long as I sat up front with her and we went slow.

Remarkably, the inexperienced driver did end up driving the group home safely. Another example of an attempt at influence through harm-minimization, this one unsuccessful, is drawn from an Oklahoma student's account:

> They then asked me if I would like to join them in smoking a cigarette. I declined their offer, of course, and while they tried many times to convince me that it would cause no harm and that it would be fun, I stood my ground. I eventually left, because the odor of the cigarette smoke got to be too much for me to handle. In this case, their negative influence was unsuccessful.

The second subtype of harm-minimization was to minimize the chances of legal penalty or negative consequences on one's grades or school performance. The example below involved one friend trying to convince another to shoplift. The student wrote:

> Since M always must "scratch by" with what she has, K suggested she just take what she wants from a store. "It's really easy. Don't you know most stores keep their cameras off? They're just for show." . . . K continued, saying "We get things taken from us everyday. It's time you started taking back from others" and "Don't be chicken. Are you really gonna go through life scared?"

As did many of the 2009 students' papers, this account exemplifies multiple forms of influence, including ridicule and one of only two accounts in all of our data to mention any sort of "neutralizing" technique to minimize the immorality of a behavior.

Another example of the minimization of legal consequences is drawn from an Oklahoma student's response:

> Me and my friend Ted work out a lot, and so we drink a lot of protein. Milk is a very important component for protein shakes, and can get expensive after going through gallon jugs within a few days. One day, we were eating lunch in the cafeteria together. I went over to

the cereal bar to pour myself a bowl when I saw two unopened, gallon jugs of milk sitting in the cooler under the cereal bar. I told Ted about this, to which he encouraged me, "Take them, nobody will see." I have yet to decide on taking them, but his influence has definitely been heavy on my mind.

An example from the 2009 Rhode Island papers is interesting in the amount of time the youths seemed to spend arguing and debating whether or not to climb onto the roof of a local store:

> We noticed that it was possible to get onto the roof of the Benny's building and all we needed to do was climb a fence onto a smaller roof and then hoist ourselves up to the top. This turned into an argument between the four of us because two of them wanted to do it and two of us did not (me included). Mark and Collin (the two that wanted to climb) decided to go without us and made it on top of the roof without any trouble. While atop the building Mark and Collin tried their best to convince Chris and me to join them. We argued for about five minutes but they convinced us that nothing bad could possibly happen to us while up there. After a few minutes of internal debate we decided to climb up with them.

There were also a number of students who gave accounts of minimizing the potential negative consequences on grades or schoolwork. One respondent wrote about two such cases that occurred when she was in high school, and gave her own take on how the influence occurred:

> For fun one day we invited him to lunch with us, which involved leaving campus and missing a class. We did this to test him and see if we could talk him into coming, which we were able to do. We appealed to the fact that we never get caught, which for most of us was true . . . There was another time when we used peer pressure on one of our own group of friends after she had promised along with the rest of us to cut a full Friday of school . . . she tried to cancel on us by telling us one of her teachers had moved a test to that day and that she couldn't afford to miss it. . . . We . . . assured her that it would be easy to schedule a make-up for the test if you had a valid reason for missing it. We told her we would take care of the reason for her and everything would be ok, at which point we were finally able to convince her to go through with her promise of coming with us.
>
> I feel that in these two cases, both individuals were afraid of the penalties they could get for doing what they did, and it took more than just the offer of "being cool" so to speak to get them to break the rules. It also took reassurance that they wouldn't get in trouble/caught for what they were doing.

Several other examples are drawn from the Oklahoma sample:

> Goose is on probation for doing drugs the previous summer, he has random drug tests but hasn't had one in a long time. Maverick asks if Goose wants to smoke some weed and encourages that it will be out of his system before the next test. Goose ends up smoking weed with Maverick, and doesn't get tested.

> The OU [redacted] team players bragged about cheating on their papers to their adviser and gave each other pointers on how to do it and get away with it.

> Last semester, some guys in my class and I got pretty good at planning out who would take notes so that one of us could skip class. It didn't always work out so well, because we always forgot to email out the notes we had taken. We all got decent grades in the class (nothing below a B, I think) so I guess it worked well enough.

> I was trying to decide if it was worth it to go to a class and my friend encouraged me not to go, saying I could learn everything from the powerpoint online.

Finally, it is noteworthy that there were only two examples in all of our data of people minimizing the moral wrongness of a deviant behavior to try to convince someone to engage in the behavior. One example is noted above, the student who wrote that stealing is okay because they were victims of theft frequently. Another was drawn from an Oklahoma student:

> My cousin punched his fiancé and choked her and then half of my family told her she was in the wrong for calling the police because he was already on probation. This just basically told him that domestic violence is okay and he can get away with it.

Clearly, the student writing this account did not agree with the attitude set forth by his or her family, and it's not an example of peer influence on behavior, but given that it was one of the few examples in our data, we thought it worth mentioning here. It's clear from our data that students in these samples did not exert influence on each other by teaching each other moral values supportive of deviant behavior. Of course, the situational accounts that we requested from our respondents might overlook processes of influence on norms or values that might be acquired over time in the course of a friendship or other relationship. Our finding that peer influence toward deviance often involved simple invitations is also consistent with the idea that norms supportive of deviance were learned prior to the time of our data collection. However, it is surprising that so few of our accounts included any discussion of morality or values, even those in which respondents were describing initiation into a deviant behavior they had never participated in before. In other words, it doesn't seem like internalized norms or values are the primary obstacle to be overcome by peers who want their friends to engage in deviance with them.

Entertainment of Onlookers

The last major category of specific influence techniques refers to the encouragement of deviant behavior for the amusement, entertainment, or other benefit of the influencers or onlookers. This category is a bit different from the previous ones because it really taps into the motivation of the person trying to elicit deviant behavior rather than the specific method of influence. We suspect that the frequency of this motivation is probably higher than our data reveal, since most students' accounts did not address the issue of the motivation of the influencer. This is also likely true for some of the other seldom-mentioned categories such as "deviance loves company" (described later). To the best of our knowledge, this motivation for peer influence has never been reported in the literature or suggested by other researchers. However, it was fairly common among our 2012 sample with 14% of specific influence incidents classified in this category (but only 4% in the 2009 sample.) Not surprisingly, encouraging one's peers to engage in deviant or danger- ous behavior was often related to alcohol use, either in encouraging excessive drinking itself or when peers encouraged intoxicated friends to engage in dangerous behavior. Some illustrative examples follow:

> At a party everyone was drinking heavily, and my peers decided it would be fun to get my friend Johnny exceptionally drunk. He ended up staying at my house because he was too intoxicated to leave. This negative influence was successful because he was seriously intoxicated and needed to be taken care of for some time.

> A group of friends found out that one of my friends had never been drunk enough to puke, so we tried to get him that drunk by mocking him for not being able to drink enough, etc. We called him names and pressured him until he was very drunk, but he didn't actually throw up.

> During April a fraternity member B came over to fraternity E house and knocked on the door. Fraternity member from B punched the fraternity member from E at the front door and ran back to his house. After the assault the fraternity member from E walked over to fraternity B and asked what that was about. After talking through a window another member from Fraternity B emerged through the shadows and punched the fraternity member from E in the back of the head giving him a concussion [sic], all because his buddies thought it would be funny.

> I do not go to bars, but I have several friends that get drunk nightly. I know this story from them coming into the dorms around 3am. One girl kept drinking till she was dangerously drunk, yet people continued to buy her drinks because they found her actions amusing. Another girl even recorded the night and posted it to Youtube.

> At a recent party, two people became drunk and started "mock" fighting. Their friends just stood around them and cheered them on. It became pretty serious after they punched a hole in the wall of the apartment complex. Now the hostess of the party is left with a somewhat costly repair.

> Post-finals week celebration at our fraternity house: one of the members was belligerently drunk and was encouraged by other members (several of which were completely sober) to start throwing around full trash bags and/or destroy one of the room doors that was already slightly damaged. The belligerent drunk, of course, then went into a destructive rampage and made the hallways look like a landfill (the dark side of Greek life . . .). Meanwhile, a few other members tried to stop what was going on, but found themselves outnumbered by the instigators and audience. They gave up trying fairly quickly. Fortunately, no one was hurt when large chunks of wood door flew down the hallway.

There were several somewhat disturbing accounts of people trying to influence others to engage in deviant behavior for their own sexual gratification, such as the following:

> A couple of friends were going to leave a party when a guy with a snake showed up. One of my friends wanted to hold it and the guys said that if they showed him their boobs then he would, so the one flashed him and tried to get her friend to do so too, but she didn't.

> I have been to parties where, of course, there have been those people, mainly guys, who try to get girls drunk in order to take them home with them. They do their best, and when

she's gone enough to not realize what's really going on, the "nice boy" she met at the door is just so "kind" enough to let her crash at his place.

I saw my roommates get girls intentionally drunk so they could take advantage of them.

One respondent added a comment on the quality of "friends" who encourage each other to engage in deviant or dangerous behavior:

> [At a party in the woods] Later in the night when they decided to let this kid drive, he drove his car down a wrong path down a hill deeper into the woods. Luckily he had a four wheel drive explorer, but the kids in the car were enjoying his mishaps. They continued to egg him on as he tried to reverse his car, breaking headlights and taillights on trees and stumps. They made it out of the woods and home without any legal issues, but what sorts of friends treat each other in this manner?

While it's clear that behavior like that described above is not motivated by caring or concern for the person being influenced, it's important to consider the role of alcohol in such instances, which often leads youths to engage in behavior that may be harmful to themselves as well as to their friends. Nevertheless, this kind of negative influence portrays a very different picture of peer influence than that implied by subcultural or learning perspectives that envision delinquent groups as close-knit groups characterized by strong bonds of mutual respect. At least for these types of situational influences, the lack of concern for peers is more apparent in our data, consistent with the control theory perspective. As Gottfredson and Hirschi (1990) argue, those most likely to engage in crime and deviance tend to be "selfish and thoughtless," although they may also be "fun to be with; they are certainly more risk-taking, adventuresome, and reckless than their counterparts" (1990: 157).

This conception of the nature of those who engage in delinquent behavior is consistent with previous literature that highlights the "fun" aspect of much deviant behavior (Goff and Goddard 1999). As Briar and Piliavin (1965: 36) put it, delinquent behavior is often the result of a situational opportunity to "get kicks," which they note is also consistent with the fact that much delinquency is non-serious, and for most youths, confined to a brief period in the life course.

Deviance Loves Company

A few of our respondents also described the motivation behind negative influence attempts as a desire for companions to engage in deviant behavior with the individual doing the influencing. As with the previous category, we suspect that if we had asked specific questions about why peers try to get each other to engage in deviance we would have uncovered many more instances that could have been classified into this category. One example illustrates this with a rather conforming behavior:

> Bee wanted dessert. Ay didn't want dessert but Bee didn't want to eat dessert alone. So, Bee talked Ay into having a dessert. It was quite tasty.

As Costello (1997) notes, teenagers rarely engage in leisure activities such as eating out or going to the movies alone. Warr (2002: 82) notes that teenagers exhibit "extraordinary sociability," and at an age where fitting in is so important, it's not surprising that youths have a strong desire to engage in mutually enjoyable activities with friends, whether legal or illegal.

There were several other examples that were somewhat different in character, where an individual wanted to drink or use drugs but apparently felt that engaging in these behaviors alone was unacceptable or stigmatizing. For example:

> The more I smoked [marijuana], the more I enjoyed it. I even pressured some of my friends to do it with me. I know it was wrong, but I didn't want to be a "stoner" and smoke alone. I even let my friend's 11 year old brother smoke with us.

> I work at a golf club and I constantly see members encouraging other members to continue to drink past their tolerance level, because you know what they say, "misery loves company." They want to have fun and drink everyday without feeling bad about it, so they peer pressure others into doing the same thing so they don't feel bad about themselves. Working at the club and serving drinks to people who literally drink everyday, has greatly changed my views on drinking. I barely drink anymore because of it.

These excerpts get at the idea that mutual engagement in activities somehow serves to sanction those activities as being acceptable, even though both of these accounts seem to indicate private realization that the behavior is not acceptable. The diffusion of responsibility concept seems applicable here as well. This concept is usually applied in cases where the presence of others seems to indicate "immunity from sanctions" (Gottfredson and Hirschi 1990: 209) or "diffusing the moral responsibility for blameworthy acts" (Warr 2002: 62). Although the behaviors our respondents describe above are "victimless" crimes, it seems that engaging in them with others removes or reduces the stigma that they perceive as possible results of their behaviors. Getting others to engage in substance use seems to normalize the behavior for the individuals engaging in it, perhaps making them feel less guilty for doing something they feel that they should not be doing.

Fear of Loss of Status

Status concerns as motivation for delinquency have received a great deal of attention in the literature over the years, with some theories, such as Cohen's version of strain theory, positing the status-enhancing function of deviance as being a primary cause of deviant behavior. As Cohen put it, "Nothing is more obvious from numberless case histories of subcultural delinquents that they steal to achieve recognition and to avoid isolation or opprobrium" (1955: 27). Status concerns stemming from the need to avoid victimization may motivate deviant behavior related to the "code of the street," where projecting a tough-guy image is crucial (Anderson 1999). And ridicule, discussed previously, is clearly related to status because ridicule threatens the target's status.

The examples in our data that we classified as fear of loss of status generally involved someone deviating so that they would maintain the quality of their relationship with others. For example:

> A classmate asked me to show him and some of his friends how to do an assignment. I knew that I shouldn't, but I helped them anyway because I didn't want them to be angry with me.

> At a party last year, I was strongly encouraged to drink, especially by those who were them-
> selves already drunk. Many people said they felt that I was judging them because I didn't
> drink. It was not successful in getting me to drink, but it was successful in reinforcing my
> general dislike of parties.
>
> A few weeks ago one of my girlfriends was pressured into trying pot for the first time by
> her boyfriend. I could tell she didn't want to and suggested we leave, but she didn't want to
> disappoint him so she smoked anyway. She smokes regularly with him now so I don't go to
> their house anymore.

Although we cannot make any definitive conclusions about the motivation of the influencers in these instances, it seems likely that they were motivated by self-interest—in the first example, the influencers were trying to get help on an assignment; in the second, the influencers seemed to feel uncomfortable drinking around someone who was not drinking, so they may have been motivated by their desire to minimize discomfort; in the third, it may be that the boyfriend wanted company in his deviant behavior. In these cases then, the desire for status is quite different from what Cohen and other cultural theorists posit as a status-enhancing function of deviance—rather than being motivated by a desire to achieve status in a group with countercultural or subcultural norms, these attempts to avoid loss of status are more the result of manipulation on the part of a self-interested other.

Finally, it's important to consider the overlap between status concerns and some of the other categories in our coding scheme, notably ridicule and emulation of admired models. As Warr (2002) notes, ridicule, status, and loyalty are likely related in the real world of social interaction, and our classification of ridicule and other coercive tactics as separate from status likely minimizes the extent to which status concerns motivate deviance. The frequency of ridicule in our data suggests that for some types of behaviors, participation in deviance seems to be a requisite for participation in parties and other group activities, and to some extent fear of loss of status as a member of the group motivates this participation. As discussed in some of the cases classified as emulation of admired models, we also found that even when failure to participate in deviance might not be sanctioned, youths perceive that they must engage in those behaviors to be accepted as an equal-status member of the group. Given the nature of our data, we cannot determine which process is actually more important in motivating conformity to group behavior, and we see this as an important avenue for future research. Looking further into the motivations of the influencers in situations like this will be especially important.

Miscellaneous Types of Influence

Several types of influence were rarely mentioned in our data, and these included four references to group deviance being motivated by boredom, three references to competition or dares motivating deviance, one case of encouraging deviance in a peer to make oneself look better in comparison to the deviant individual, and one case in which a driver was insulted by a passenger wearing a seatbelt so the passenger removed his seatbelt to avoid insult to the driver. In the case of boredom, three out of the four influence attempts were also classified as an additional type of influence, but boredom has often been mentioned as a motivating factor in youths engaging in deviance, so it was recorded as an additional category here. We were surprised there weren't more references to competition given the prevalence of beer pong and other drinking games among young people, but it appears that the desire to beat one's peers at these games is not a salient factor in motivating their participation given how seldom this was noted in our data.

Conclusions

It is clear from our data that peers can and do have causal influences on each other's deviant behavior, and it is not safe to conclude that the peer effect is merely a result of self-selection in which "birds of a feather flock together," as control theorists typically argue (Hirschi 1969; Gottfredson and Hirschi 1990). However, the types of influence that were reported most frequently in our sample were not of the sort we would expect from differential association or learning theories of deviance, which hold that norms or values conducive to deviant behavior are learned through interaction with deviant peers (Burgess and Akers 1966; Sutherland 1947). The most common type of influence in our 2012 sample was for peers to provide a simple offer or opportunity for deviant behavior, in many cases by offering drugs or alcohol or issuing an invitation to join them in a deviant activity. This type of trivial causal effect of peers on delinquency is consistent with self-selection, particularly when an invitation to deviance is readily accepted. This type of opportunity effect is also consistent with the image of the offender portrayed in self-control theory (Gottfredson and Hirschi 1990) and opportunity-based explanations of crime such as routine activities theory (Cohen and Felson 1979; Osgood et al. 1996). In these conceptions, offenders are assumed to be driven by a situational desire to maximize pleasure and minimize pain, with little concern for the long-term consequences of the behavior. Crimes are seen as easy, trivial events that occur without advance planning and without much motivation on the part of the offender. These views are consistent with our respondents' reports of peer influence often taking the form of simple offers or invitations to participate in an activity. However, our focus only on situational influence on behavior means that we cannot rule out the possibility that prior learning of deviance norms leads to the ready acceptance of deviant invitations. Even in those cases in which respondents are engaging in a deviant behavior for the first time, though, we saw little evidence of norm transference in our respondents' interactions.

On the other hand, our results also uncovered some types of peer influence that may be more in line with subcultural explanations of the peer effect, in which deviations from the norms of the larger culture are seen as normative within the group under consideration. Quite a few respondents reported that they engaged in alcohol or drug use because they thought it would help them fit in with an admired crowd. They at least perceived that the behavior was considered desirable in that group, even if this perception may not have been entirely accurate. It was not the case in these instances that there was any overt reinforcement for the behavior or overt threat of punishment for not engaging in the behavior, so these accounts were not entirely consistent with traditional learning theory explanations of crime like Sutherland's or Akers's theories that view acceptance of deviant norms as the key cause of deviant behavior. Rather, these cases are more in line with Jones's (1964) concept of ingratiation or the idea that conformity to peers' behavior can occur without the private acceptance of that behavior (Warr 2002). These cases present interesting avenues for further research, and potentially for prevention programs designed to reduce deviant behavior, as some programs have done with regard to reducing alcohol abuse among college students (Perkins, Haines, and Rice 2005).

We also found the use of various coercive tactics of peer influence to be fairly common in our sample, which is also, at least on the face of it, more consistent with learning theories than control theories. The typical attempt in our data to coerce friends into engaging in deviance used ridicule, specifically referring to someone as childish ("don't be a baby") or threatening someone's masculinity (the use of the term "pussy" was fairly common). These influence attempts, which were often centered around drug and alcohol use, seem to reflect a norm of "partying" among people of a certain age or status. In some cases, these interactions seemed to tie one's masculinity to the willingness or ability to take risks, which again seems to suggest that risky behavior is normative among certain groups. One question that remains, however, is why individuals are motivated to coerce their peers into engaging in these deviant behaviors. In at least some instances described in our data, the motivation appears to be a selfish one, such as the case in which passengers in a car were ridiculing the driver for not being willing to make an illegal U-turn—they wanted the driver to turn around, and when he didn't do so quickly enough, they used coercive tactics to get him to do what they wanted.

Another type of influence attempt revealed in our data, influencing friends toward deviance for the entertainment of others, also suggests selfish motivation for peer influence. Clearly, encouraging already-intoxicated friends into drinking even more is not motivated by concern for their wellbeing, nor is encouraging a friend to drive a car through the woods or to punch someone in the head.

We were surprised at the frequency of behavior that could accurately be described as "peer pressure," particularly given that both social learning theorists and control theories summarily dismiss it. As noted previously, Warr thinks it appropriate only for casual barroom conversation. Akers holds that overt pressure in the form of threats of ostracism or ridicule are only "marginal factors" in social learning theory (1998: 66). Gottfredson and Hirschi argue that empirical evidence "flies in the face of" the idea of peer pressure as an important cause of deviance, since delinquent youth are less, rather than more, concerned with their friends' opinions of them (1990: 158). We believe that the dismissal of peer pressure as an important type of influence on deviance is the result of the fact that criminologists haven't collected data that adequately tap into the situational dynamics of deviant acts. Gottfredson and Hirschi assume that concern for others' opinions in a general sense is necessary for peer pressure to occur, but that level of concern is not necessary to explain why someone might take a drink in response to a roomful of peers chanting "Drink!" or a carload of teenage boys calling a friend a "pussy" or "baby." It also seems clear that these kinds of group processes do not teach values that support crime, they merely force someone into doing something that they do not want to do. This finding might help explain why association with deviant friends is correlated with delinquency even when most social influences most people face are conforming. How can the influence of parents, teachers, and most other adults be overcome by the influence of a few delinquent friends? It may simply be that youths are often coerced into doing things that neither they nor their parents or teachers approve of.

From our perspective, it is not at all surprising that these kinds of situational pressures lead individuals to engage in deviant or criminal behavior. It is, we think, more interesting to ask why peers would pressure their friends into deviant behavior like this when they clearly do not want to join in. Although we did not explicitly ask our respondents to report on their motivations for trying to influence their peers' behavior, we think it will be important for future research to do so, in part to try to understand these motivations. Some of our findings suggest that these motives are selfish, which is more consistent with the control theory view of offenders as not being very good friends than with learning theories' view of them. But given that we did not ask our respondents to report on motives, we'll leave this as an open question for future research to address.

Notes

1. Because one incident may have been coded as two or more types of influence, our use of percentages to describe the frequency of different types of influence attempts is actually the "percentage of codes" rather than the "percentage of incidents" or "percentage of influence attempts."
2. We have reproduced students' comments verbatim, maintaining spelling and other errors, throughout the book.
3. Although the narratives from the 2009 URI data collection tended to be more detailed than URI and OU data collected in 2012, the respondents did not provide much detailed information about the nature of the relationship between the parties involved in the incidents, in spite of the assignment instructions specifically asking for that information.

4

MECHANISMS OF POSITIVE INFLUENCE

As noted previously, there has been almost no attention in the criminological literature on positive peer influence, and we believe this is a major oversight in the field. The "peer effect" in criminology has essentially been seen as synonymous with negative or pro-deviant peer influence, and the delinquency/peer delinquency correlation is generally taken as evidence for normative and social learning theories and against alternatives like social control and routine activities theories. Although some research notes the potential for alternatives like simple opportunity effects (e.g., Felson 2003; Osgood and Anderson 2004), most studies that find a relationship between delinquency and peer delinquency over and above self-selection conclude support for cultural deviance or learning theory explanations (e.g., Haynie 2001; Matsueda and Anderson 1998). This is often true even when these studies fail to include measures of norm transference, despite the fact that this is the central causal mechanism in learning theories that link contact with deviant others to the individual's deviance. It seems that learning theories of crime "own" the peer effect (Costello 2010).

It is time that cultural deviance and learning theories' ownership of the peer variable is challenged. With the focus in social control theory on the causes of conformity rather than the causes of crime and deviance (Hirschi 1969), social control theory is a likely starting point. Because social control theory assumes that human nature is fundamentally asocial or selfish and that crime and deviance provide their own rewards, the theory does not view crime as problematic. Rather, the theory asks, "Why don't we do it?" (Hirschi 1969: 34). Hirschi (1969) focused on attachments to others, including friends, as providing indirect controls on our behavior. If we are strongly attached to others, we care what they think of us, and we will be less likely to engage in behavior that they would disapprove of. Because control theory assumes a common value system in society and explicitly denies the existence of "deviant subcultures" or groups that positively value criminal or delinquent behavior, Hirschi argued that deviant behavior is disapproved of even by those who engage in the behavior themselves. Thus, attachment to others gives us something to lose by committing crime, which is the positive regard of our friends, relatives, and associates.

Hirschi's focus on others as providing indirect controls on behavior through the individual's concern for others' opinions may have led him to neglect consideration of the possibility of peers providing direct controls on each other's behavior. Despite the fact that control theory focuses on why people don't commit crime, even Hirschi failed to consider the possibility that peers can directly *prevent* each other from committing crime, beyond what we would expect as a result of self-selection (e.g., the lack of opportunity for deviance experienced by youths with conforming friends). This was likely due in part to his focus on addressing the claims of the dominant theories of the time, such as Sutherland's differential association theory and Miller's (1958) conception of a lower-class culture as a cause of delinquency. Much of Hirschi's analysis of the peer effect in *Causes of Delinquency* tested hypotheses generated from learning explanations of delinquency against the idea of self-selection, and he concluded that weakened social controls preceded delinquent friendships and delinquent behavior. This focus may have guided subsequent criminological research in a similar direction, causing researchers to focus on the negative influence versus self-selection dichotomy and therefore overlook the possibility of direct control from peers.

As discussed in Chapter 1, however, there has been some attention paid to the issue of positive peer influence in the psychological literature and the literature on children's friendships. In their review of the literature on adolescent friendships, Berndt and Murphy (2002: 79) conclude that the idea that friends' influence on behavior is predominantly negative is a "myth," and instead state that friends' influence is typically toward conforming behavior (Costello 2010). Youniss and Smollar (1985) hold that like adult friendships, children's friendships are based on mutual trust, caring, and loyalty. Further, they note that the focus in much of the literature on youths conforming to deviant peer expectations is misguided, that "a different kind of conformity is typical of friendships," conformity to principles that "represent a set of basic values that pertain to social cohesion since they call for tempering of the self in concern for the other person" (1985: 134; also cited in Costello 2010). One of Youniss and Smollar's adolescent respondents viewed peer influence in this way: "You have to talk to your friends, you can't always go to parents. A friend can keep the other from doing something wrong" (Youniss and Smollar 1985: 129; also cited in Costello 2010).

Cairns and Cairns (1994) followed two cohorts of children over a period of 14 years to study a wide range of developmental processes and outcomes, including aggression and crime. They reach similar conclusions, and state that:

> Peer influence gets little respect. It is commonplace to blame peers for deviance, delinquency, drugs, dropout, and other developmental disasters. Yet peer influence is rarely credited for good things, including the transmission of moral values, academic excellence, and courageous acts.
>
> *(1994: 90)*

Studies of children's friendships have revealed that friends can have positive effects on each other's academic performance (Epstein 1983) and behavior in school (Berndt and Keefe 1995), and that they can "actively discourage" drug use and sexual behavior (Clasen and Brown 1985: 454). They also provide social support for each other, which may reduce deviant behavior (Colvin, Cullen, and Vander Ven 2002). Some research finds that peers perceive "pressure" both toward and away from deviant behavior (Brown, Clasen, and Eicher 1986; Clasen and Brown 1985), with many adolescents reporting experiencing more pressure from peers away from bad behavior than toward it, especially among younger children (Clasen and Brown 1985). Similarly, Flanagan, Elek-Fisk, and Gallay (2004) found that children, especially younger children, are willing to try to prevent friends from smoking, drinking, or using drugs, and that this was more common among girls than boys.

Another body of research applicable to the issue of peer social control has focused on the situational correlates of violence. For example, there is evidence that witnesses to disputes can prevent imminent violence (Black 1993; Felson 1982; Felson and Steadman 1983; Oliver 1994) or have the opposite effect and instigate violence (Cooney 1998; Felson et al. 1994; Felson and Steadman 1983). However, this body of literature focuses more on the structure of the situation and neglects consideration of the individual characteristics of those involved and mechanisms of influence. For example, the gender composition of drivers and passengers in cars has an effect on speeding and dangerous driving (Simons-Morton, Lerner, and Singer 2005), but we know little about how and why this happens.

There is also a small body of research that has focused on intervention in drunk driving situations. This research has shown that college students quite frequently intervene when faced with a situation in which someone is about to drive while drunk (Rabow, Hernandez, and Watts 1986). Estimates of attempts to prevent drunk driving in the general population range from 30% to 60% in a one-year period, and one study of college students found that 68% of students faced with this situation reported trying to prevent the act (Hernandez, Newcomb, and Rabow 1995). Conceptualizing these influence attempts as altruistic or helping behavior, Rabow et al. (1990) studied the decision-making process involved in such situations. They found that intervention increased when people perceived the target as in need of help, when they felt able to help, and when they knew and liked the target of intervention. Interestingly, they found no effect of a feeling of moral obligation to help, and no gender differences in the likelihood of helping.

Despite the existence of a body of literature demonstrating positive peer influence, the only research in criminology that systematically focuses on a direct preventative effect of peers on deviance is that based on Sampson and Laub's age-graded theory of informal social control (1993). Sampson and Laub argue that delinquent trajectories begun in childhood can be altered by turning points in life, such as acquiring a good job and/or developing an attachment to a spouse. Their study of formerly delinquent men found that attachment to a wife is negatively correlated with adult crime, and they suggested that wives can limit criminal opportunity and provide "continuity in guardianship" that tends to prevent crime (1993: 143).

Laub and Sampson's later work (2003) also focused on marriage as one turning point among formerly delinquent men, with the men who desisted from crime being more likely to have stable marriages than those who persisted in crime. They note that for the men who were strongly attached to their wives, marriage had a positive or conforming influence on routine activities, provided social support, and provided direct social control that reduced men's opportunity to engage in crime, drinking, and other potentially counterproductive behaviors. They also note that wives in their sample helped keep men away from deviant peers, as in the case of their respondent Leon, who said that one of his former friends had committed a murder on a night when ". . . I had a date with my wife and we went to a dance. If it weren't for my wife, I'd probably be up for murder" (Laub and Sampson 2003: 121).

Laub and Sampson (2003) note that one surprising finding in their research was the extent to which the wives in their sample provided direct social control over their husbands' behavior. This included setting rules for the number of hours a husband could spend drinking in a bar with friends, making sure their husbands got up and got to work even when they had been out drinking the night before, and, as in the case of their respondent Leonard, forcing him to choose between his friends and her (Laub and Sampson 2003: 136).

It is interesting that in some of Laub and Sampson's (2003) discussion of the positive influence of wives, as in Warr's (1998; 2002) discussion of the issue, "wives" are distinguished from "peers" as if wives are not peers or friends of the individual. For example, Warr (2002) argues that the negative correlation between marriage and crime is caused by the decrease in deviant peer association that is associated with marriage and not by the effect of marriage, or the influence of the spouse. Here, the implication is that the important causal factor is the *absence* of deviant peers rather than the *presence* of a conforming peer, the spouse. While this is to some extent merely a semantic difference, we believe that it once again points out that attention has been paid only to negative peer influence, while the possibility of positive peer (or spousal) influence has been mostly ignored.

Thus, despite the general lack of research focused on adolescent peer influence toward conformity, there is evidence in the literature that peers can influence each other in positive ways. Friends can keep each other out of trouble and can encourage each other toward positive, prosocial, and productive behavior. The extent to which this happens, the causes of positive influence, and the effectiveness of positive influence attempts are not known, and we begin to explore these questions below.

Methods

The data presented below were collected with the same methods as described in the previous chapter—a set of papers completed by first-semester URI freshmen in 2009, and open-ended questions on a survey completed by URI and Oklahoma students in 2012. In this case, however, students were asked to describe an incident of positive peer influence they directly witnessed or participated in. The students were asked to describe an incident in which they were the "influencer" or the "influencee," and the influence attempt could have been away from deviant behavior such as drinking and driving, or toward positive or prosocial behavior such as going to class or completing an assignment.

After reading the 2009 papers carefully several times, it was clear that most of the coding categories used to analyze negative peer influence could be used to analyze the positive influence attempts, with some modification. Although it was not a primary purpose of this research to directly compare the two types of influence, we thought it would be useful to use similar categories for positive influence attempts to see if there were any similarities or differences in the techniques students were using to try to influence each others' behavior.

As we did with the responses to the open-ended questions on negative peer influence, we analyzed the 2012 URI and Oklahoma students' responses separately to determine if there seemed to be any patterns of difference between the two groups. One difference emerged from the two sets of responses. The URI students were less likely to report coercive attempts at positive influence than the Oklahoma students, and they were more likely to report doing good deeds for someone as an example of positive influence. These accounts included incidents like taking care of a friend who had had too much to drink, or preventing someone from being victimized by someone else. These sorts of behaviors do not really tap into what we were most interested in measuring, but because they were examples of prosocial behavior directed toward peers and they

TABLE 4.1 Positive influence mechanisms, Oklahoma and Rhode Island 2012 samples and Rhode Island 2009 sample

Influence Type	2012 Sample		2009 Sample	
	N	Percent★	N	Percent★
General pressure/influence	340	62%	22	25%
Emulation of admired models/setting a good example	9	4%	7	10%
Simple offer or invitation	47	22%	7	10%
Maximizing potential consequences	58	28%	25	37%
Coercive tactics	79	38%	20	30%
Benefit of onlookers	4	2%	1	1%
Conformity loves company	0	—	2	3%
Fear of loss of status	0	—	2	3%
Taking care of friend/preventing victimization	10	5%	1	1%
Other	2	1%	2	3%
N's	549		89	
N's excluding general pressure	209		67	

★ Percentages for categories other than general pressure or influence are calculated excluding general pressure or influence

were reported more than a few times, we recorded them as their own category. Overall, though, there were no striking differences in the types of behaviors the two groups were reporting, either in terms of the type of behavior that was being influenced, or the mechanisms by which these influence attempts were happening.

The frequencies of positive influence mechanisms are reported in Table 4.1. One interesting finding is simply that there were so many positive influence attempts described by our respondents. The 2012 survey had a total of 549 classifiable incidents (compared to 422 for negative influence as described in Chapter 2), and there were 89 classified from the 2009 papers (compared to 69 negative influence attempts). The numbers, excluding the "general pressure or influence" category, are also larger for positive than negative influence, with a total of 276 positive influence attempts across the two study years compared to a total of 189 negative influence attempts. Clearly, criminologists are missing a great deal of information by studying only negative peer influence.

Positive Influence Mechanisms

As seen in Table 4.1, similar to the findings for negative influence, most students' comments in the 2012 data were too general to classify beyond the "general pressure or influence" category, with 340 of the 549 responses (62%) so classified. As with the negative influence measures, the 2009 student papers were much more detailed and therefore easier to classify into more specific categories. Only 22 of the 89 comments (25%) in the 2009 papers were classified as general pressure or influence. Some examples of responses coded as "general pressure or influence" from both 2009 and 2012 include the following:

A few of my friends were arguing over trivial things and ended up angering each other. They decided they were going to fight to resolve the issue but my friends and I convinced them that it was a huge overreaction.

One of my friends began to more heavily become involved with smoking marijuana and it dramatically altered her priorities. Her future fell to the back burner and her main priority was getting high. When it came time to decide on what college we were going to attend she just said she was not going to go. It had then become apparent that we had to step in because we knew that this is not what she really thought or wanted it was just the pot talking. We sat her down and explained to her what we were seeing and we helped her to get her life in order. This was a successful experience that I encountered with positive peer influence.

For the past couple of weeks, I've been trying to help my friend in leading a healthier life by taking care of his body. He doesn't get enough sleep, he doesn't eat healthily, and he procrastinates way too much. I try to persuade him into changing some of his habits to better himself, but in the end, it never works. He continues to do the same things, and he has become more dependent on me instead. My influence has not been as successful as I would want it to be.

I had to convince a friend of mine a couple of weeks ago to stop skipping class because his grades were suffering. He did end up going to class more, so the influence was successful.

Similar to the language used in the general category of negative influence, common words and phrases here were "convinced" someone to do something, "encouraged" someone, "argued" with someone, and so on. We also saw several examples of respondents "calming someone down" when they were angry, "warning" a friend against engaging in a behavior, or "reprimanding" someone for doing something wrong. As with the negative influence attempts, many of the behaviors the students mentioned dealt with drug and alcohol use, driving under the influence, and attending classes or doing schoolwork. Although many of the behaviors discussed were rather trivial in nature, there were several examples of respondents reporting helping others out in very significant ways, such as the example above of a group of friends who encouraged a friend to attend college.

Emulation of Models or Setting Good Examples

A total of 16 of our respondents recounted incidents in which they were positively influenced or served as a positive influence by either behaving like their peers or trying to set a good behavioral example for their peers. Four percent of the 2012 sample and 10% of the 2009 sample reported such influence, which is fewer than reported this process for negative influence (8% and 18% respectively).

One student wrote about her younger sister, whose grades had started falling in high school. The student talked to her sister about trying harder in school, and she noted, "She has also made a lot of new friends in her classes who study just as hard as she does and make her want to try even harder. It really helps to have a good group of friends." This comment is interesting in that it focuses on the positive influence of friends rather than the lack of negative influence from friends, and thus it provides a good example of the kind of influence that has been largely ignored in the criminological literature.

My roommate and I have a very stable relationship and are on the same page as pertains to school work and personality. She is a hard worker and whenever she is writing a paper or taking notes,

> it influences me to likewise study for an upcoming test or do homework that might not be due for a few days . . . when I see her studying, I don't want to disturb her and so I open up my books and review notes . . . I believe that my study habits also influence her in a similar manner.

This response is also interesting in that it hints at the quality of the relationship between the two roommates—although the student does not mention the level of attachment between the two explicitly, there is clearly mutual respect between the roommates that facilitates, in this case, positive influence. Other examples include:

> Taylor was getting out of shape. The group decided to start working out together to give her the motivation to lose weight.

> I'm a pretty good christian guy, so I have friends that cuss practically every sentence. When they are around me though they don't, although they occasionally slip.

Another student's account demonstrates both setting a good example and pointing out the negative consequences of behavior to his friend:

> My roommate Flynn has skipped class A LOT lately. He hasn't gone to all of his classes almost all semester. He sleeps until 1 or 2 everyday, and only eats and plays basketball and video games when he is awake. He seems careless about his grades and personal health. Me and my friend Ted have been encouraging him to attend class, study, and get into better shape physically. We nag at him, explain to him the ramifications of his choices, and give him examples from our own experiences. I still don't know if he gets the message, but he at least recognizes that he's doing something wrong now.

Another example that hints at the quality of the friendship:

> There was a big exam coming up, and Nick decided to stop smoking for the week before to prepare. Seeing this, Juan also decided to stop smoking for the week, for solidarity. However, the next week they picked the habit back up.

These examples are interesting in that the students seem to have a pretty good sense of the potential positive impact of group behavior and social support for positive, conforming behavior. As has been well documented (Mermelstein et al. 1986; Resnick et al. 2002; Wing and Jeffery 1999), social support can increase health-promoting lifestyles and can help change negative health behaviors like cigarette smoking. It might be useful for criminologists to consider ways of exploiting the tendency of at least some youths to try to promote positive behaviors in each other, rather than simply focus on educational campaigns to reduce deviant or unhealthy behaviors.

Simple Offers or Invitations

As with negative influence, it was fairly common in our sample that respondents made offers or suggestions to their peers that provided them with the opportunity to avoid deviant behavior or to engage in positive, conforming, or prosocial behavior. Twenty-two percent of the 2012 comments and 10% of the 2009 comments were classified as simple offers or invitations, which is somewhat less common than the frequency with which these processes were mentioned in the negative peer influence responses.

The key difference between statements classified as "simple offers or invitations" and those classified as "coercive tactics" is the degree of forcefulness expressed. For example, the first statement below was written by a student in the 2012 sample, and was coded as a simple offer or invitation; the second statement was classified as a coercive tactic.

> I stopped my friend Janice from driving drunk to a party. Instead, I didn't pregame [drink before going out to a bar or social event] so I took the initiative to be D.D. [designated driver].

> Drinking at my friend's house a couple months ago. We took another friend's keys and made him stay over, since he had too much.

In the first statement, there's no indication that the respondent had to exert any real pressure on her friend to let her be designated driver, it seems that she merely offered and the offer was accepted. In the second statement, the terms "took" and "made him" both imply that there was more than merely an offer to allow the student to stay over, so that statement was coded as a coercive influence attempt.

Many of the examples in the category involved drinking and driving, such as these:

> Joey was way too drunk after the movie and Emac offered to drive him home. Joey readily agreed without a second of thought put to it. Joey had just almost fallen down the stairs and didn't recognize how intoxicated he was until that moment. Joey did not want to drive drunk he stated and thanked Emac, repeatedly as all good drunks would do.

> I was with a group of friends drinking, and we were trying to decide who was going to drive us to a party, when one of our group suggested we get a cab, since everyone had already been drinking. We ended up taking a cab.

> One of my friends met a girl at a party we were at. He was taking her outside for some fresh air and to talk, but she looked really uncomfortable about the situation. Those of us in the kitchen asked them to come inside and talk to us instead. We didn't think he intended her any harm, but we wanted to make sure he didn't do anything he would regret in his drunken state. They both came back inside and we all enjoyed each others company.

These cases demonstrate how easy it can be, depending on the individuals involved, to prevent deviant or dangerous behavior simply by suggesting a safer or wiser alternative. Another respondent made this point him- or herself, and also offered a comment on desired qualities in friends:

> [At a party] One kid in particular was way too drunk to drive home. He didn't think so. He mumbled, "I just have to drive down the street." Some people said oh yeah that's true he doesn't have to drive that far. One kid said no way that's dumb. Let me drive my friends home then I will come back and take him. It seemed so simple. Here all these people were going to let this drunk kid drive and it took just one person to do the right thing. I was shocked. It was good to see. It made me think to myself, now that's a friend you want to have.

A few comments coded into this category involved the refusal to help someone engage in deviant behavior, such as this example:

> My boyfriend's roommates asked us to buy them alcohol although they are underage, we said no therefore they didn't drink that night.

Finally, several examples in this category focused on encouraging prosocial or positive behavior rather than avoiding deviant behavior:

> Janice suggested that Mildred join the intramural softball team, as it would be a good experience for her. She stated reasons such as the possibility of getting to know more people, to become closer to those you do know, also it would be fun and you'd be getting active. This was successful. This was not exactly preventing negative behavior, but rather encouraging good behavior.

> The problematic behavior wasn't so much the problem. What happened was my friend invited me to go running with her and I said yes and am now into running on a regular basis. Thus I have now become more active and exercising more.

> One of my friends was finding it difficult to focus and study for his final exams. So I invited him to come study with me in the Library (since I am there ALL the time). He agreed and ended up getting a lot of work done. The hardest part was not getting distracted and getting on Facebook or texting his girlfriend, but with some encouragement he managed to focus. He left there wondering why he didn't go to the library more often during the semester, so I would say the "influence" was successful.

These kinds of influence attempts point out an interesting avenue for further research on peer influence, which is the study of who, how, and when attempts at influence toward positive behaviors (as opposed to the avoidance of negative behaviors) occur. We begin to explore these questions in Chapter 5.

Coercive Tactics

As noted above, accounts classified as coercive used language that indicated more than simple invitations to engage in (or avoid) a particular behavior. Coercive tactics were more common for positive influence than negative influence, with 38% of the 2012 sample reporting "positive" coercion compared to 20% reporting "negative" or pro-deviant coercion, and 30% of the 2009 sample reporting positive coercion compared to 20% for negative coercion. Common terms used in accounts classified as coercive include some of the same phrases we saw in the negative influence accounts, such as "made me." The positive coercive influence accounts also often referred to "taking" someone's keys or an alcoholic beverage away from them, "keeping" someone from doing something, or physically restraining someone by "holding them back" from a fight or physically wrestling someone's car keys away. These comments are illustrative:

> Jill and Brittany were at a party at a frat house. Jill, who has a boyfriend, wanted to go home with Bobby, a frat boy. Brittany tried to remind Jill of her boyfriend, but Jill really wanted

to go hang out with Bobby. Brittany told Bobby to just put his number in Jill's phone, and then made Jill leave the party with her.

Joe and John were upset at each other. They started yelling at each other and said things like "Do you want to fight?" I stepped in and took Joe out of the room. There was not a fight.

There was a group hording a game during a party at my house. One of my roomates was able to set up a list that you had to sign up on and calmly got the others to either agree to it or leave. They ended up leaving, and the game kept going pretty well all night.

The accounts below were typical of many accounts in which friends did not let friends drive drunk:

One of my friends was at a party and he wanted to drive home after drinking. A group of us said no and blocked the door and took his keys. We were successful at stopping him and my friend got a ride from someone else.

A friend at a party took another friends keys in order to stop them from leaving the party drunk. The drunk friend was mad at first but the next day was very glad their keys were taken.

As in the latter example above, it was not at all unusual for students to write about their friends becoming angry with them when they tried to stop someone from driving after drinking, and it was also common for them to report their friends thanking them the next day when they had sobered up. In contrast to many of the examples we classified as "simple offers or invitations," then, these examples point out how difficult it can be to exert positive influence on someone, particularly when he or she is intoxicated.

As with the coercive attempts at negative influence, there were several subtypes of coercive positive influence that emerged from our analysis of the data. These were, in order of frequency, physical intervention such as restraining someone from fighting, taking someone's keys away or wrestling them away, coercive appeals to loyalty, tricks, threats, and ridicule. The frequency of use of different types of coercion was different for the positive influence attempts than for the negative influence, particularly in that ridicule was used much less often for positive influence than for negative, and physical intervention and appeals to loyalty were used more often for positive influence. Each of these is discussed below.

Physical Intervention

The most common method of coercive influence is perhaps the simplest—physically restraining someone from doing something, going somewhere, or physically taking away someone's drink or car keys. Fourteen of our respondents reported this type of influence attempt. The two examples below were typical:

A friend of mine tried to drive home drunk after a party one night, however before he could reach his car a group of his friends wrestled him to the ground and took his keys so he couldn't drive.

At a party, one of my friends saw her enemy and wanted to fight her. Instead of allowing my friend to fight, I held her back and moved her to a different area of the party.

One respondent described an incident that is probably quite familiar to any sports fan, and he also provides his take on the nature of "true" friends:

> I play soccer weekly in an indoor league and fights occur frequently because of how overcome with emotions players let themselves get. Recently, during a game, a teammate of mine was physically hit by a player on the opposing team. His brother witnessed the event and immediately started towards the instigating player, however, the entire team ran out and pulled him onto the bench in order to prevent the situation from escalating any further. Unfortunately for players on another field, a fight escalated to the point of physical harm, and many people were arrested and taken to jail. I understand the act of pulling someone off of the field to prevent a fight is not directly influential on their behavior, but I think it speaks volumes about the kinds of friends a person surrounds himself with. The team was willing to stop the incident at the origin in order to prevent any further conflict, and that probably saved many a trip to jail for no important reason other than a transient emotional flare up.

As noted previously, although many of the incidents students wrote about were somewhat trivial, there were some notable exceptions to that pattern, such as this story about a young man, Nick, who was developing a serious prescription drug addiction:

> My brother loved Nick and hated seeing him this bad so he took it on to himself to get Nick help, even though Nick always denied having a problem . . . . My brother met up with Nick one day and basically beat the crap out of him because that's the only way Nick would get it through his head that my brother was dead serious . . . after my brother did what he had to do Nick told his parents what was going on and they ended up sending him to get help in a place in Florida. Nick has now been clean for a year and is better than ever, he is planning on going into the air force and is planning on becoming a pilot.

Only one example of physical intervention involved trying to get someone to engage in positive behavior rather than to avoid or stop a deviant behavior:

> Amy had been working on a 10 pg paper for the past two days. She'd gotten little sleep and finally passed out. Tammy let her sleep for a few hours then came and told her to wake up and finish her paper so it wouldn't be late. Amy got up and started working on her paper again.

It was interesting that this subtype of coercion was the most common for positive influence and was essentially absent in our descriptions of negative influence. There were many coercive attempts at negative influence that were not specific and might have involved physical force, but no students reported physically forcing someone to engage in deviance or beating anyone up in order to convince them to engage in deviant behavior. This is in contrast with some accounts of gang delinquency in which membership requires an initiation such as being "beaten in" or forced to go commit a particular type of crime (Decker and Van Winkle 1996). Even in those cases, though, the coercion is designed to result in membership in the gang but not necessarily any specific deviant behavior—failing to complete the initiation resulted in failure to become a member of the group. Based on our (non-representative) data, then, we conclude that physical intervention is a common method of coercing someone to stop or avoid a deviant behavior, but rarely used to coerce someone into committing a deviant act.

Coercive Appeals to Loyalty

The second most common subtype of positive coercion tactics was coercive appeals to loyalty. This method of coercion occurred only rarely for negative influence, but was reported by 11 of our respondents for positive influence. The example below is similar to some examples of the use of threats to encourage conformity (discussed below), but because there was no overt threat to end the relationship, it was instead classified as a coercive appeal to loyalty:

> I entered a new relationship a few months ago. Previously, I had done drugs occasionally—ecstasy once, and pot a few times. When I expressed my desire to try ecstasy again, my boyfriend didn't forbid me from doing it, but made it clear it was something he wouldn't be very pleased with. Because ecstasy is not that important to me, I decided to forego any opportunities to take it in order to keep my relationship stable.

The example below also taps into friends' loyalty in the sense that one friend is trying not to scare the other:

> I have a friend who is a reckless driver and he does not like to wear his seat belt. Every time I ride with him, I'm scared and always tell him to drive slower and put his seat belt on. He usually slows down and puts his seat belt on because I told him to and he knows that I am scared, but when he is by himself, he's reckless as can be without his seat belt.

Another respondent reported a group of friends trying to get another friend to stop using marijuana, all through phone calls while they were away at different colleges. She writes:

> Whenever Susie called each of us, we would ask her if she is still smoking marijuana and if she was, most of the long distance conversation would be dedicated to pleading her to stop because it is not a habit that she would be starting in college. Some of my friends would refuse to pick up her calls or only speak to her once on a weekly basis because they were upset with this new experimentation of hers. Most conversations would involve us saying, "Susie, you need to stop smoking weed. You know that its bad for you, and you shouldn't be one of those bums who smoke it constantly in college. We are your friends, and we're only looking out for you". . . For one month, she ignored all three of us and continued smoking weed. This positive peer influence was an attempt but failed when Susie decided to continue this habit of smoking marijuana.

Only one of the positive influence attempts of this type was focused on getting someone to engage in a prosocial behavior rather than to stop engaging in deviance, and that involved a group of friends trying to get a friend to attend confirmation classes with them at their church. The respondent wrote:

> Mark said to him, "Come on, Andrew, take Confirmation class with us. We'll go to the prayer groups together and sign up for the same service projects." I added, "Sure, Andrew, you'll be bored and miserable, but at least we'll be together" . . .

Tricks

Ten respondents reported using tricks to get someone to stop engaging in a deviant behavior. Several of these dealt with trying to prevent a friend from drinking to excess or driving after drinking, such as the following:

> At a date party, one of my guy friends was way too drunk. Me and my friends knew how much he had drank and were already afraid of possible alcohol poisoning so we hid his alcohol from him and went out to the store to buy sparkling grape juice and cider. When we got back to the frat house we had pulled off the labels from the bottles and made him think that what he was drinking was wine. Because he was so drunk he believed us and carried the bottle around like it was wine. Later that night, when he went to bed we turned him on his side and took turns watching him throughout the night. We took him to the bathroom to throw-up and changed the clothes that he ruined. The next morning he apologized and thanked us for our help.

> He was determined to get in his truck and drive home, which is about 25 minutes away. I was not going to let this happen. I asked him for his keys and he refused to give them to me. I tried snatching them out of his hands, but he is two feet taller than me, so it was very hard to do. Finally, I asked him if I could move his truck because it was in the way of my car. He let me do this and I pocketed the keys.

These examples again point out how positive influence can be fairly easy, and suggest that tricking an intoxicated person might be a more effective method of positive influence than other coercive methods, which can lead to stubborn refusals of help.

One of our first-year URI students recounted an incident that happened when he was in high school:

> When he told me he was going to "tag" the side of the school . . . I laughed at him, thinking he wouldn't do that. After school . . . I couldn't find Fred anywhere. Little did I know, he was on the side of the school building, with a few cans of paint . . . He shook the can, pointed it to the wall, and was ready to spray. Just then, I put my acting skills to the test and yelled, "Get out! A teacher is coming!"

This attempt at positive influence was effective, as the respondent and "Fred" ran away without committing the crime.

Threats

Seven respondents mentioned the use of some sort of threat to influence someone's behavior in a positive direction, all of which focused on getting someone to stop or not engage in a deviant behavior. Several respondents threatened to end a friendship or dating relationship if the target of their influence attempt used drugs, continued to drink to excess, or smoked cigarettes, and these attempts were reported to be successful or partly successful. For example, one of our URI respondents told of a circumstance in which she had told her friend Ashley that she would use ecstasy with her. When she told her friend Jake about the plan,

He totally flipped out on me and told me we would not be friends if I popped pills. He told me I could die taking it once. He told me he was not having me ruin my life just to fit in. After thinking about what he said I really thought about how stupid I was being. Usually other people's opinions don't affect me but after hearing it out of his mouth it clicked. I told Ashley that I didn't want to do it; I didn't want to risk dying just to do drugs. She was pissed at me but I felt amazing after standing up to her . . . she probably still does drugs but not in front of me anymore.

This account also demonstrates the use of multiple tactics of influence, since Jake not only threatened to end the friendship, but also pointed out the potential negative consequences of using the drug. The final comment in this response is also interesting in that it demonstrates a type of self-selection—Ashley might still use drugs, but seems to avoid doing so in the presence of someone who disapproves of the behavior.

Another example of the use of threats involved the threat of physical violence if someone didn't follow dorm rules about not throwing food garbage away in a common restroom:

. . . some people still committed such bathroom atrocities as before, but were now confronted by other people who had since stopped . . . this part of the dorm had some rather large college athletes residing in it who did not want any infractions against them due to their sporting activities and the implications it might have for them, so . . . they would yell at, insult, and/or threaten the individual committing [the bathroom crimes] until they reversed their negative behavior.

This account was the only report of using threats for somewhat self-interested reasons—the respondent's assessment of the athletes' motives is that they wanted to avoid punishment for the messy bathroom, and we speculate that having to live with the mess might also have been a motivation of those confronting the offenders.

Ridicule

One difference between the positive and negative influence attempts was how relatively infrequently respondents mentioned ridicule when trying to influence their friends positively. There were only four such events recounted by students across both samples, two from the URI 2009 data and two from the Oklahoma sample. (Recall that ridicule was the single most common mechanism of negative influence described by the URI 2009 sample, even more common than the general influence or pressure category.) Some examples follow:

I have a friend who is really bothered by my weight and eating habits. Last semester she invited me to go workout with her and I did. I changed my eating habits and I went to the gym everyday. However, this semester my course work is harder so I am spending more time studying and I can't workout everyday. EVERY TIME I see my friend that is the first thing she says to me. "Jill, have you been working out regularly?" I always tell her no and I know it bothers her that I have not been working out. This positive peer influence just gets on my nerves and frustrates me. She brings it up all the time and even in front of other friends she tells me I look bad and I would look better if I worked out. I appreciated her concern at first, but now I am just embarrassed when she mentions it or I feel frustrated because I don't have time like last semester to workout.

I was recently around two of my husband's friends who I very seldom see, but when they are not out drinking and "hitting campus corner," they're talking about "epic times when we played beer pong." They are extremely intelligent people who can waste their free time doing whatever they want because they can make the grades without trying. We were at a wedding reception and there was a child at our table listening to them talk about their alcohol consumption. I told them to shut up and grow up. As one might expect, my influence was not successful.

It is interesting that ridicule is a common negative influence tactic among our respondents but not a very common positive influence tactic. We speculate that this may be because the stakes are higher in the positive influence scenarios—when one is trying to prevent someone from doing something that is potentially fatal such as drunk driving, individuals do not want to risk ostracizing the person whose behavior they are trying to influence. It may also be that it's difficult to effectively ridicule someone whose behavior is consistent with that of those in the same social setting. If everyone at a party is drunk, it's difficult to effectively ridicule one's friend for being drunk (and it may be difficult to make a drunk person feel the effects of ridicule as well). However, if everyone at a party is drinking except one person, it may be much easier to effectively ridicule the "odd man out."

It's also likely that the motivations for negative influence are more selfish, such as when one person is viewed as being judgmental for not joining the group in their deviant activity, or when someone is trying to get someone to join them in substance use so they don't feel stigmatized for drinking or using drugs alone, as discussed in Chapter 3. If the motivations to influence are selfish, the individual may be less concerned for the emotional reaction of the person he or she is trying to influence, and be more likely to use a relatively cruel method of influence such as ridicule. If the motivation for influence is more other-oriented or altruistic, however, it would be inconsistent to use an ostracizing form of influence such as ridicule. Because we did not explicitly ask respondents to report their motivation for influencing their friends, we cannot answer these questions with our data.

Maximizing Negative (or Positive) Consequences

Another very common type of attempt at positive influence is maximizing negative consequences of deviance or maximizing positive consequences of conformity or prosocial behavior. This was the single most common method of positive influence in our 2009 sample, with 37% of incidents being classified in this way, and the second most common of the specific influence tactics in our 2012 sample with 28% of incidents fitting this category. As with the negative influence attempts, there were three main types of consequences invoked by those trying to influence someone's behavior: penalties, including legal penalties, bad grades, or getting into trouble at school or with some other authority figure; physical harm, such as harm to one's health or property or to one's mental health; and pointing out the moral problems with a behavior.

Making reference to potential physical harm was the most common of the three subtypes in this category, which is not surprising given the preponderance of influence attempts related to drug or alcohol use, including cigarette smoking and dangerous driving practices, whether under the influence or not. The following examples were typical:

My friend keeps nagging me to stop smoking cigarettes and even has sent emails with pictures of cancer patients and smokers lungs but it does not do any good.

I told my friend to quit smoking cigarettes because she has a history of cancer in her family. She smokes when she is stressed and ironically, she is usually stressed about her mom's cancer. She finally listened to me and bought patches to help her quit. She's still struggling with it, but it's a step in the right direction.

Talking to a friend about eating healthier, because he is gaining too much weight. We have mentioned to him several times. Although he didn't change too much his behavior, he seems more aware and concern.

After a friend's 21st birthday at his apartment we wanted to go to the pool. We were all intoxicated and the friend whose birthday it was had already passed out. We thought about carrying him with us because we didn't want to leave him alone. Another friend, who was the least drunk of anyone at the apartment, convinced us that leaving the apartment while carrying our passed out friend to the pool would be too dangerous, and we decided to stay inside instead.

My friend Lindsey has a tendency to drink too much. This is especially bad because she has Hep C and it does compromise her liver. Whether we go out and drink or hang out and discuss past evening events, I always ask her to drink less and inquire about her Hep C checkups and status. She makes and follows through with the appointments once I remind her and thanks me. When we do go out together I keep a watchful eye on her and remind her to tone down her drinking because I won't be there to always take care of her and there are people who can and have taken advantage of her intoxicated state.

Some of my friends wanted to race back to the dorms in our cars from someone's house and a few of the people discouraged that and convinced them not to because it is dangerous and something bad could happen.

There were several examples of respondents pointing out the negative consequences of hard drug use, including the example above in which our respondent's friend Jake warned that taking Ecstasy even once could lead to death, and the example below, which pointed out a health problem that "Steve" apparently thought was just as bad:

Steve used to do a lot of blow. Now he just smokes weed a lot and drinks occasionally. Steve was hanging out with Bob and Steve offered to find some cocaine to kill the boredom. Bob spent the next 20 minutes listing negative aspects of cocaine use. Ultimately, Bob pointed out the problem of long term impotence. Steve relented and they just drank a couple of beers and smoked a bowl. Steve ended up apologizing to Bob and admitting that nobody likes a junkie. Hard drugs are bullshit.

While most of our drinking-related responses dealt with negative consequences of drinking and driving, one of our Rhode Island respondents reported an experience of friends drinking while boating, despite his warnings:

About two hours into the trip [on a boat], a friend of one of my friends . . . pulled out a 12-pack and a small bag of marijuana . . . he asked me if I wanted a drink, and I decided to try to inform him on how dangerous the situation of drinking on a boat. I had specific examples, telling him the story of the young man in Barrington who was drinking on a boat. The alcohol, mixed with horseplay, resulted in the death of his friend. This was one example of when my positive influence was not successful.

Like the previous example, there were several examples of positive influence attempts in which the respondent referred to specific examples of death resulting from dangerous behavior, such as this one:

Recently, I was able to get one of my friends to agree to walk to destinations following alcohol consumption. I had just explained that a friend of mine died in January from driving drunk, and I don't want to run that kind of risk.

The second-most common type of negative consequence mentioned was legal or school-related problems. Among the 2012 respondents, skipping class was the most commonly discussed deviant behavior in this category, as in these typical examples that seem to fit squarely with Gottfredson and Hirschi's (1990) self-control theory:

My roommate frequently skips a class he has in the morning of Mondays, Wednesdays, and Fridays. My other roommates and I tell him constantly he should go since last semester he did the same thing and failed a class. He admits he should put more effort into the class but still skips it.

Recently one of my friends has been skipping classes very frequently and it is negatively effecting her grades. Several of my friends and I have pointed out that her GPA and scholarships will be effected if she doesn't make any effort to go to class. However, even though she agrees in principle she hasn't started going to class.

There were also a number of cases in which students reported concern over being arrested as a method of positive influence:

A cop came to a house party and a few people were upset that the party got busted so they began heckling the policemen from a different room. I told them to keep quiet in order not to make the situation worse and after a minute of reasoning they let it go and were silent.

The example below, from the URI 2009 sample, points out a number of different types of both positive and negative influence attempts—the respondents' friends were minimizing the potential negative consequences of theft, the respondent is invoking his own moral thoughts about the behavior but not using those to try to convince his friends that it was a bad idea, and instead maximizing the potential negative consequences to his friends to try to influence them. He is also demonstrating the effect of perceived norms, in that he thought his friends would think he was cool if he committed the theft with them.

My friends thought it was a good idea to steel food from the store. "It will be a lot cheaper because we won't have to pay any money and no one will find out," they said to me. At first

I got nervous because I didn't want them to make fun of me for not wanting to take part in stealing. I've been brought up to obey the laws and it just felt wrong. They didn't see the harm in steeling a few things. Finally after a few minutes I got up the courage to stand up for myself and tell them that it sounded like a bad idea. I thought of what all of our parents would say after getting a call from the police station or what would happen if we got caught. It all wasn't worth it to me. I wanted to do it just to prove to them that I was cool but I felt too guilty. I talked them out of it by asking them what the point was and what if we get caught. Then they realized that it was a stupid thing to do. After negotiating with them we left the store with nothing.

There were several other examples from our 2009 sample of the kinds of concerns high school students have about getting into trouble or not being successful in school.

> . . . my phone started ringing and it was Lisa's mom telling me that I needed to get Lisa home immediately . . . we dragged Lisa home kicking and screaming. Later while at the party I got a call from Lisa. She was saying how she was going to run away from home and come to the party. Knowing this would only make things worse I convinced her to stay home . . . later she told me she was glad she stayed at home instead of running away because it would have ruined her and her moms relationship.

> My friends had the idea of drinking before the last football game of the season. I had the vibe that we would get caught, which would deter us from being able to play a part in senior activities . . . I told them that it is not worth losing being able to play a part in senior activities just because I made the decision to drink before a football game. They started to think about what I had said and realized that what I was saying was 100% true . . . come to find out, people who did drink before the game lost senior privileges and totally regret the fact that they made the decision to drink.

Another example involved a group of kids who were considering breaking into a yacht owned by the family of a friend of one member of the group. The respondent continued:

> They continued to try to convince Ke and me that this was a terrific idea; "it'd be so fun, and how badass would it be to say we broke onto a boat?!" said KI. Ke said something along the lines of "this is a horrible idea. What if we get caught and can't get into college because of this?" I could definitely tell K and C were thinking twice about it after Ke said that, and she continued, asking K if she thought L [the friend whose family owned the boat] would be mad at us if we tried to do something that dumb. K and C seemed to be considering it, but told us they were going to try to take the boat anyways. Ke was furious, and ended up leaving and driving home. Not too long after that, M and I drove home as well. Later we found out that they left soon after us. My guess is that the reason the positive influence worked was because K and C were afraid of what Ke would think of them if they continued with a plan that none of us "approved" of.

This account again demonstrates multiple types of positive and negative influence, and helps demonstrate the somewhat complex situational dynamics involved in this fairly mundane example of attempted influence.

Finally, the least frequent type of consequence mentioned in this category was moral consequences, with only 10 respondents invoking the immorality of a behavior to try to influence their
friends.

> During lab check-out for Chemistry, a friend was missing a beaker and wanted to take one
> out from a drawer that belonged to someone who didn't go to check-out. I told him it wasn't
> fair to the other person. He didn't really care and took it anyway.

The following attempt at moral influence seems to have backfired at least temporarily:

> A while back, I revealed to my fair-trade, organic friend that I had been eating at Burger King.
> She told me not to do that, but she was judgmental that I just wanted to do it more. (Granted,
> I also find such things generally icky, and have since stopped, but if anyone's to blame for that,
> it's Michael Pollan, not her.)

Surprisingly few of our respondents wrote about academic dishonesty, the following was an
exception:

> I tutor and have a student who asks me to write papers for him for money. I obviously deny
> him, but also try to make himself realize it's immoral and that he will never learn if he does this.

Another student in our 2009 sample wrote about an incident that happened in high school, when
she and her friends learned that another friend:

> . . . had been stealing clothes and little accessories when she was with her other friends
> she made at her high school. Neither of us thought that shop lifting was okay and we
> knew that our friend didn't either. We confronted her about the shop lifting and we got
> upset with her when she openly just told us that she was doing it and seemed to be okay
> with it. She acted as if there was nothing wrong with stealing. After talking to her and
> telling her that we thought that was wrong and that we knew she was a better person
> than that, she became feeling guilty because she knew that we she was doing was morally
> wrong and by law illegal. She finally agreed with us that she needed to stop and that she
> wouldn't do it ever again.

As with the negative influence attempts, then, there were relatively few appeals to morality as a
method of peer influence toward positive behavior. At least as evidenced in our sample, then, it
doesn't seem that moral values are an important, salient feature of situational peer influence on
behavior (although it's likely that they play a role in selection of friends). The implications of
this finding for the value-transmission explanations of deviance are clear—at least as far as our
data indicate, convincing someone that they can "get away" with a behavior is a much more
commonly used method of peer influence than is trying to convince someone that a behavior is
acceptable or excusable. For positive influence, convincing someone that they cannot get away
with something also seems more typical than convincing someone that a behavior is morally
wrong.

Again recognizing the limited scope of our data, our findings also lend support to the perspective that there is a single, universal set of norms and values that guide behavior as opposed to the relativist view that norms and values vary widely across groups. At least in our sample, there is clear recognition of the harm that can result from deviant behavior, whether it's physical harm to one's health, potential legal consequences, or consequences to one's life chances. This supports the view that the potential harm that can result from behavior is a key determinant of its perceived "acceptability," and that even those who engage in deviance recognize the harm that can result from such behavior (Costello 2006a; 2006b).

Benefit of Onlookers, Conformity Loves Company, and Fear of Loss of Status

These categories are included as separate categories in Table 4.1 mainly for comparison with the categories listed in Table 3.1, as they occurred infrequently in the positive influence data. While influencing one's peers to do deviant things was mentioned fairly frequently as a form of amusement or entertainment, it seems that getting someone to do something more conventional is not as amusing, as we would expect. There were a few examples of respondents trying to get their peers to engage in conforming behavior for their own benefit, including one who encouraged the person who was driving him not to drink, and this respondent who also needed a ride:

> Roommate wakes up late. We have the same class together and he's my ride. He complains that he is out of fucks to give and doesn't want to go to class. I urge him to go; he goes. Seems pretty successful to me.

There were also a couple of examples of people who were being taken advantage of by someone's deviant behavior, so by refusing to continue being taken advantage of, they had a positive influence on their friend's behavior. One example is:

> Bill had been covering for Darla during Chemistry class. Occasionally he would earn clicker points for her, while she skipped class. One day though, Bill saw that Darla skipped class to get on Facebook. Bill confronted Darla about it, and they both came to the realization that Darla had been pushing her problems onto other people and had been taking advantage of Bill. Bill offered to support her with her school work, and be there for her with her relationship issues with Norbert, but he would no longer earn Darla her clicker points if she decided to skip class. Darla and Bill are now both happy and are studying hard to do well on the Chemistry final.

As we speculated with regard to negative influence, we suspect that the kinds of events that fit under the "conformity loves company" classification are underrepresented in our data—people do conforming things with peers all the time, but those kinds of mundane events were not really represented in our data. One of the two examples in this case involved a girl in high school who was not going to drink at a party so encouraged her friends not to either, and this kind of influence would be unlikely to be reported in most cases when non-drinkers spend time together.

This points out that positive influence in the sense of preventing deviance requires someone in a peer group to suggest or initiate deviance in the first place, which is unlikely to happen in very conforming groups of peers.

Finally, although status and loyalty clearly overlap to some extent, there weren't many examples in our data of the fear of loss of status motivating conforming behavior. One example was provided above in the anecdote about the group of kids who were thinking about breaking into someone's yacht—the respondent said that the kids decided not to do it in part because of what other friends would think of them. Research on social control theory suggests that these kinds of concerns may be more common than they appear in our data, to the extent that attachment to peers is negatively correlated with deviance (Hirschi 1969). Because we were looking for evidence of peer influence away from deviance, the opportunity to influence someone's behavior positively requires someone to instigate deviance in the first place. Thus, self-selection probably limits the frequency of positive peer influence in the sense that very conforming peer groups lack such instigation.

Other Categories

There were a number of other incidents described that didn't quite fit our existing categories or our conception of positive influence. In particular, 11 respondents described situations in which they helped someone else, took care of them, or prevented them from being victimized. These didn't really fit our conception of positive influence on behavior because there wasn't a clear reference to a specific deviant behavior that was prevented:

> On a Friday night, john decided to go drinking. He got pretty drunk but his friends, who were not drunk, took the time to make sure he got home and took care of him. If they did not do this he may have ended up dead or doing something even more dumb than just drinking.

In some cases, events classified in the "taking care of a friend" category didn't fit our conception of peer influence because the person whose behavior the respondents were trying to influence wasn't really a friend but seemed to be a stranger.

> Person A was being fooled around with by two other people. His roommate saw what was happening and got them to stop.

> One of my friends witnessed an incident of sexual harassment on campus and decided to intervene. A recently broken-up couple was having a public fight, and the man grabbed the woman several times and attempted to follow her home. My friend prevented the man from following her by threatening to call the police.

> I had a friend who was mocking another friend because of a failed relationship, but another person stepped in and stopped him.

> While leaving campus corner after a night of drinking a few friends and I saw a man yelling at his girlfriend in her face in an alley and she was crying. A guy friend of mine tried to intervene and we got some police officers involved to stop it. We could have just ignored it but we didn't.

These cases are interesting to consider in light of recent attention being paid to ways to prevent bullying in schools and to prevent sexual assault on college campuses. It is clear that peers and bystanders sometimes do intervene to prevent criminal or deviant behaviors, and it will be important for future research to try to learn more about when this is likely to happen and how to encourage it.

Conclusions

Our major conclusion from this analysis is that "positive peer pressure" is very real, it has prevented countless deviant, dangerous, and criminal behaviors, and it has no doubt saved lives. Despite the fact that our sample of college students cannot be taken as representative of any larger group, there is enough anecdotal evidence in our data to support this general conclusion. Positive peer influence might be even more common than negative peer influence, as it is in our data. Clearly, then, criminologists are missing a wealth of information on crime prevention, and social science in general is overlooking a powerful type of influence on behavior.

The most common types of influence away from deviance or toward positive, prosocial behaviors were the use of coercive tactics, emphasizing negative consequences of deviance or positive consequences of conformity, and a simple opportunity effect. These three techniques were also commonly reported methods of negative influence. One difference in the use of coercion for positive influence is that ridicule was rarely used to try to influence friends' behavior positively, but it was a common method of negative influence in our data. Although we did not ask respondents to report on their motivation for trying to influence their friends' behavior, we speculate that positive influence attempts might be more altruistically motivated than are the negative influence attempts, which is consistent with the finding that ridicule was used less in positive influence attempts.

In light of the theoretical issues we've explored thus far, one of the more interesting findings is that we've seen very few references to values in our respondents' accounts. When friends try to influence each other toward deviance, they are more likely to try to assure each other that they won't get caught or experience other negative consequences than they are to try to reassure each other that there is nothing morally wrong with the behavior in question. When they try to influence each other away from deviance, they are similarly much more likely to point out the potential negative consequences of the behavior, such as physical harm or legal sanctions, than they are to invoke moral standards against the behavior. As we noted previously, we cannot make any general conclusions about peer influence on norms and values over time from our data, since they are by design measuring situational processes. However, the overall pattern in our data is quite consistent with the results of other research that finds more of a direct effect of peers' behavior on the individual's behavior rather than an indirect effect through attitude transference (Warr 2002; Warr and Stafford 1991). Our research also provides support for Warr's (2002) contention that those who engage in deviant behavior are at least aware of the norms of broader society and aware of the consequences, including "moral condemnation," they might face as a result (2002: 62). Taken as a whole, then, our research provides little support for cultural deviance or learning theories of crime (Burgess and Akers 1966; Sutherland 1947), and little support for notions such as Sykes and Matza's (1957) that definitions of deviant behavior as unacceptable must be rationalized or neutralized before deviant behavior is possible. Rather, at least some of our evidence is more consistent with social control theory's (Hirschi 1969) focus on peers as a source of conforming influence, albeit not necessarily through the indirect mechanism of concern for friends' opinions. As Laub and Sampson (2003) found with regard to wives' control over husbands, there is a surprising level of direct control of peers on each other's behavior.

Our results suggest that we have much to learn about positive peer influence, including the following: When does it happen, who does it, and under what circumstances? Are certain types of people more likely to try to influence their friends' behavior positively or intervene in a potentially dangerous situation? When are peer influence techniques likely to be more or less successful? We begin to address these questions in the following chapter.

5

EXPLAINING PEER INFORMAL SOCIAL CONTROL

Our findings from the qualitative analyses in Chapter 4 clearly show that college students do try to positively influence one another's behavior—both by trying to prevent deviant behavior and by encouraging prosocial behavior—through a variety of mechanisms. Important questions remain, however. Who is likely to use positive peer pressure? When is it more or less likely to be effective? Below, we address these issues by testing hypotheses derived from social control theory and self-control theory with survey data collected from our URI and Oklahoma samples.

As we discussed previously, both social control theory (Hirschi 1969) and self-control theory (Gottfredson and Hirschi 1990) predict that offenders are likely to have poor social relationships. For social control theory, offenders have weaker social bonds than non-offenders. A weak bond in one respect is associated with weak bonds in other respects—youths who have weaker bonds to parents, for example, are likely to have weaker bonds with peers. If individuals do not care much about their parents' opinions of them, they are unlikely to care about their friends' opinions, their success in school, and so on. For self-control theory, offenders tend to be self-centered and lack concern for others. They are not the kinds of people who make good friends—they are unreliable, selfish, and impulsive (Gottfredson and Hirschi 1990). Although they might be a lot of fun to be around, they are not the kinds of people one can count on when one really needs a friend.

Thus, control theories predict that young adults who are more constrained by the forces of both social and self-control should not only be less likely to engage in deviant behavior, but should also be more likely to attempt to steer their peers away from such behavior, and to encourage them to engage in prosocial behaviors (Costello 2010). We also expect that as a result of self-selection, individuals who report a greater level of attachment to their friends are likely to have friends who are also attached to them. Thus, those with higher levels of social and self-control should be more likely to be the targets of informal social control attempts from their friends. Additionally, we expect that those who are more "sensitive to the opinions of others" (Hirschi 1969: 16) will be more likely to actually change their behavior as a result of a friend's attempt at influence. Thus, we expect that the success of attempts at positive influence will be greater among those more strongly attached to their friends. Hypotheses 1 through 3 below reflect these theoretical predictions. Because individuals tend to select themselves into peer groups based on their level of deviance, however, opportunity also plays an important role. It may be that members of more conventional peer groups provide one another with fewer opportunities to exert social control. Hypotheses 4 and 5 take into account the importance of opportunity.

Hypotheses

H1: Respondents who are more strongly attached to peers are less deviant and have fewer deviant peers than respondents who report weaker attachments to peers.

According to Hirschi (1969), strong bonds to others should act as constraints on deviant behavior. Additionally, both social and self-control theories view the social bonds between deviant youth as weaker than those between conventional youth.

H2: Higher levels of peer attachment will be positively related to attempts at prosocial influence among peers and increase the likelihood that such attempts will be successful, independent of levels of respondent and peer deviance.

Stronger bonds between friends should motivate peers to look out for one another, including attempting to influence one another in prosocial ways. This prediction is consistent with Rabow et al.'s (1990) finding that degree of "affinity" for the target of influence was related to intervening in drunk driving situations. Strong bonds between peers should also translate into attempts at informal social control being successful more often.

H3: Higher levels of social and self-control will be positively related to attempts at prosocial influence among peers and increase the likelihood that such attempts will be successful, independent of levels of respondent and peer deviance.

According to Gottfredson and Hirschi (1990), those with low self-control tend to be self-centered and indifferent to the feelings of others. It follows that those with higher levels of self-control will be more likely to try to prevent friends from engaging in behavior with potentially negative consequences. There is evidence that altruistic community values are associated with lower crime rates (Chamlin and Cochran 1997), suggesting that those with stronger belief (Hirschi 1969) might be more likely to try to intervene to prevent deviant behavior. Additionally, high levels of both social and self-control should make individuals more likely to respond favorably to peer attempts at prosocial influence.

Independent of levels of social and self-control, however, those who have more deviant friends have more *opportunity* to administer control, and those who are more deviant will present their friends with more opportunities to try to positively influence their behavior. This leads to our final two hypotheses:

H4: The more deviant the respondents' friends, the more likely they are to report "administering" control, independent of levels of social and self-control.

H5: The more deviant the respondents, the more likely they are to report "receiving" control from their peers, independent of their levels of social and self-control.

From an opportunity perspective, the frequency with which individuals are presented with deviant behaviors will predict the frequency of attempts at positive influence, regardless of levels of social/self-control. This prediction is also consistent with control theory's assumption of value consensus—even those who engage in deviant behaviors recognize that the behaviors are non-normative (Hirschi 1969; Kornhauser 1978). Because the "success" of such attempts at positive influence is not affected by opportunity, however, our predictions about the success of influence attempts should not be dependent upon the level of individual and peer deviance.

The Sample

Data for these analyses were collected from the sample described in Chapter 1—the 2012 survey of undergraduate students at the University of Rhode Island (URI) and the University of Oklahoma (OU). The data collection process differed across the two schools, so we discuss them separately below.

Data from URI are drawn from a convenience sample of 108 students in a large section of a general sociology course. Students completed a paper-and-pencil survey during class time for extra credit in the course. Surveys were anonymous, with extra credit awarded on the basis of students' signed consent forms, which were separate from the surveys. The number of consent forms submitted matched the number of surveys received. Although the sample may not be representative of the student body, it is demographically similar, with 45% of the sample male, 88% non-Hispanic white, and with an average age of 19 years.

The OU survey is also based on a convenience sample of students selected in 2012. Students were recruited via mass email to the main campus undergraduate population of OU. Students were invited to fill out an anonymous survey asking about peer influence on deviance and conformity and were provided with a link to the online survey website SurveyMonkey.com. They were also informed that four study participants would be randomly chosen to win a $100 Amazon gift card.

A follow-up email was sent out two weeks after the initial email, asking students who had not yet responded, but who were interested in participating, to take part in the survey before it closed. The survey remained open for five weeks and a total of 723 students participated. Similar to the URI data collection, the OU sample was not meant to be representative of the student population as a whole, and does differ slightly from the broader undergraduate population, with females (58% vs. 50% in the university population) and students who identify as non-white (30% vs. 25% in the university population) slightly overrepresented. The average age of sample respondents is 20 years old.

The two samples were combined to produce an initial sample size of 831. Respondents with missing data on key demographic variables (e.g., sex, race/ethnicity) as well as those with incomplete surveys were dropped from the data set, bringing the sample size down to 768. All subsequent analyses use the combined sample. The complete survey is presented in Appendix B, and all of the components for the indexes used in the analyses are presented in Appendix C.

Dependent Variables

Attempts at Prosocial Peer Influence

Respondents were asked a series of questions designed to measure how often and in what ways young adults "receive" and "administer" informal social control from/to their peers.

The *receiving control* index indicates how many times in the past year a friend tried to prevent/ stop the respondent from engaging in various deviant behaviors (e.g., driving while under the influence of drugs/alcohol, cheating on a partner, or skipping classes), or encouraged them to engage in prosocial behaviors (e.g., working harder at school or exercising more). Responses were coded 1 = never, 2 = once or twice, 3 = several times, and 4 = many times. The final additive index[1] included 12 items, with a range of 12–46, a mean of 18, and a Cronbach's Alpha of 0.78. The *administering control* index measures how many times the respondent tried to prevent a friend or friends from engaging in the same deviant behaviors named above, or attempted to encourage a friend to engage in prosocial behaviors. Responses were coded as described above. The final additive index included 13 items, with a range of 13–49, a mean of 25.5, and a Cronbach's Alpha of 0.83.

"Success" of Attempts at Prosocial Peer Influence

Respondents were asked to assess the "success" of the various attempts at peer informal social control. Following each set of questions tapping administering and receiving control, the survey asked respondents to indicate how often they/their friends were successful in their attempts. Response categories ranged from 1 = "never or almost never" to 5 = "always or almost always." There was one additional response category included in each of these questions, which was "I have not tried to . . ." or "A friend has not tried to . . ." exert informal social control.

Because we do not know whether those choosing this response category actively chose not to engage in such attempts at control or were simply not given the opportunity to do so, we recoded these responses as missing data, so all analyses predicting the "success" of attempts at informal social control are, by definition, limited to those respondents who actually made such attempts.[2] The *receiving control success* and *administering control success* indexes both range from 2 to 10, with mean scores around 7, and higher scores indicating higher levels of success.

Independent Variables

Social Control Variables

Our first set of predictor variables are derived from social control theory (Hirschi 1969), and include peer, parental, and school attachment, along with belief. The *peer attachment* index is comprised of responses to three questions: "I respect my friends' opinions about the important things in life," "I know I can count on my friends to help me if I need them," and "I care about my friends' opinions of me." Response categories ranged from strongly agree to strongly disagree, with high scores indicating high peer attachment. Responses to the three items were summed to create the peer attachment index, which ranges from 5 to 15, with a mean of 13 and an Alpha of 0.70.

The *parental attachment* index is comprised of six questions asking about respondents' relationships with their parents. Response categories ranged from strongly agree to strongly disagree, with high scores indicating higher levels of parental attachment. Index scores range from 6 to 30, with a mean of 23, and a Cronbach's Alpha of 0.81.

The *school attachment* index was created from six questions about school (e.g., how much respondents like school, how hard they try, and their college GPA). All items were coded so that higher scores reflect higher attachment. Because the items comprising this index had different response categories, they were standardized prior to creation of the index. Summing the Z-scores for each item produced an index ranging from −18.39 to 7.51, with a mean of .03 and an Alpha of 0.79.

The survey included five questions tapping Hirschi's concept of "belief," including questions such as "It's okay to get around the law if you can get away with it" and "Rules were made to be broken." All items were coded so that higher scores reflect higher levels of conventional belief. Responses were summed to create the *belief* index, which ranges from 5 to 25, with a mean of 19 and an Alpha of 0.81.

Self-Control Variables

The survey also included behavioral measures of self-control tapping "risky" behaviors over the past year (e.g., traffic tickets, accidents, emergency room visits, helmet/seatbelt use). Prior research has found that behavioral measures predict deviance as well, if not better than, attitudinal[3] measures (DeLisi 2001; Marcus 2003; Piquero et al. 2005; Ward et al. 2010). Further, Hirschi (2004) has argued for the superiority of behavioral measures of self-control. Using items with loading scores above 0.45 from the factor analyses, we employ a four-item (traffic ticket; motor vehicle accident; bike/skateboard, etc. accident; emergency room because of injuries due to an accident) *behavioral self-control* index, with a range of 7 to 16, a mean of 15,[4] and an Alpha of 0.48. High scores indicate higher levels of self-control.

Despite the known problems with asking survey respondents to report on their friends' behavior, available resources prevented us from obtaining independent reports of respondents' and their friends' deviance. Given our interest in the situational characteristics of offending, this problem is likely not as pronounced in our research as it is in research specifically focused on explaining respondents' level of deviance using peer deviance as an independent variable. Thus, we asked respondents to report on the deviance of their peers, specifically how many of their friends smoke cigarettes, binge drink, smoke marijuana, skip class, and have been picked up by the police. Response categories were coded as 0 = none, 1 = one, 2 = two, 3 = three or more, and 4 = I don't know. We recoded the "I don't know" responses into the "none" category, since if a respondent is unaware of deviance engaged in by his/her peers, it is unlikely to have an effect on his/her behavior. Four items were used to create the *peer deviance* index, which ranges from 0 to 12, with a mean of 4 and an Alpha of 0.73. Interestingly, 23% of the respondents scored 0 on the scale, indicating that none of their friends had engaged in any of the behaviors comprising the index or they did not know if any of their friends had.

Study participants were asked to self-report the frequency with which they engaged in a variety of deviant behaviors. Keeping in mind that university students as a whole are unlikely to have extensive criminal histories, our questions sought to tap behaviors likely to be found among our population. Items included how many times in the past year the respondent had engaged in theft (two questions), driven while under the influence of alcohol, gotten into physical fights, and engaged in casual sex; as well as how many times in the past 30 days they had used drugs (three questions), drank heavily, or smoked. Response were coded as 0 = never, 1 = once or twice, 2 = several times, 3 = many times. The additive *respondent deviance* index ranges from 0 to 24, with a mean of 3 and a Cronbach's Alpha of 0.78. As was the case with the distribution of the peer deviance index, a substantial minority of our respondents, 36%, indicated that they had not engaged in any of the listed behaviors. Note that while 36% of our respondents indicated they had not engaged in any of the deviant behaviors listed on the survey, only 23% indicated that their friends had not engaged in any of the same behaviors. While the nature of our data does not allow us to test the accuracy of our respondents' reports about their peers' deviance, this does suggest the possibility of overestimation of peer deviance found in prior research (e.g., Turrisi et al. 2007; Young and Weerman 2013).

Table 5.1 presents summary statistics for all the variables used in the regression analyses, including standard demographic control variables. The demographics of the sample are typical for a college population. The average age of respondents is 20, and 41% of the sample is male. While 82% of the sample indicated white as their race/ethnicity, 29% indicated at least one other category (respondents were allowed to choose multiple racial/ethnic categories), with Native American and Hispanic being most common.[5] Twenty-three percent of the respondents indicated they were in a fraternity or sorority, and on average had at least one parent with a college degree or higher.

TABLE 5.1 Descriptive information for variables used in analyses

Variable	Range	Mean	SD
Age[a]	1–6	3.30	1.62
Male	0–1	.41	.49
Non-white (1=Yes)	0–1	.18	.38
Fraternity/sorority (1=Yes)	0–1	.23	.42
Parental education[b]	1–3	1.82	.83
Peer attachment	5–15	13.06	1.67
Parental attachment	6–30	23.15	5.02
School attachment	−18.4–7.5	.03	4.67
Belief	5–25	19.03	4.06
Behavioral self-control	7–16	15.33	1.07
Administering social control	13–49	25.52	6.70
Success: Administering social control	2–10	6.65	1.60
Receiving control	12–46	18.16	4.73
Success: Receiving social control	2–10	7.25	.75
Peer deviance index	0–12	4.04	3.65
Respondent deviance index	0–24	2.86	3.83

[a]Response categories: 1=18, 2=19, 3=20, 4=21, 5=22, 6=23 or older
[b]Response categories: 1 = neither parent has a college degree, 2 = one parent has a college degree or higher, 3 = both parents have at a college degree or higher

As we would expect from a university student sample, our sample is a fairly conforming group—possible scores on our deviance index range from 0 to 24, and our mean score is 2.86. Similarly, peer deviance ranges from 0 to 12 and has a mean score of 4.04. Our respondents also score high on measures of social control and self-control. Clearly, then, it is important to keep in mind that our results cannot be safely generalized to young people as a whole or to higher-rate offenders.

Results

We begin with the presentation of simple frequencies to establish that our respondents do, in fact, engage in efforts at influencing one another's behaviors in positive ways. Table 5.2 shows responses to the individual survey questions asking respondents to report on their own, as well as their peers'

TABLE 5.2 Frequencies (in percents) for peer informal social control

Variables	Never	Once or Twice	Several Times	Many Times
Administering Control				
Drinking and driving	33	40	21	6
Drinking/drug use	44	33	18	4
Casual sex	70	23	5	2
Infidelity	67	26	6	1
Fighting	71	24	4	1
Other illegal activity	63	28	7	2
Work harder at school	14	30	35	20
Wear seatbelt/helmet	34	25	24	17
Eat better	31	31	23	15
Exercise more	29	33	24	14
Unhealthy habit	29	32	26	14
Receiving Control				
Drinking and driving	77	18	4	1
Drinking/drug use	73	20	5	2
Casual sex	91	7	1	0.5
Infidelity	92	7	1	1
Fighting	89	9	1	0.3
Other illegal activity	87	11	1	0.4
Work harder at school	35	36	23	6
Wear seatbelt/helmet	71	16	10	4
Eat better	39	35	19	8
Exercise more	34	38	21	8
Unhealthy habit	73	17	8	3

attempts at preventing deviant behavior and encouraging prosocial behavior. As can be seen from the table, many of our respondents report both administering and receiving control. For example, about 67% reported that they had tried to prevent a friend from driving after drinking or using drugs in the previous year, which is virtually identical to the 68% of college students who reporting trying to prevent driving after drinking in the study by Hernandez, Newcomb, and Rabow (1995) discussed previously. Approximately 70% of our sample reported trying to get a friend to eat better or exercise more, and about 86% reported that they had encouraged a friend to work harder at school.

We found that respondents reported administering control more frequently than they reported receiving control. This makes sense given the fact that most of our respondents will be reporting on trying to control behavior of a number of friends, whereas they're only reporting for one person's experience of receiving control—their own.[6] Nevertheless, reports of receiving control were also fairly common. For instance, over 25% report that a friend tried to prevent them from drinking/drug use after they were already intoxicated, and over 65% indicated that a friend had encouraged them to exercise more. Consistent with the findings from Chapter 4, then, our respondents frequently report that they and/or their peers have actively engaged in attempts at influencing one another's behavior in positive/prosocial ways. While a substantial number of respondents report that they or their peers have not engaged in some of the behaviors (e.g. trying to prevent a fight), we cannot determine if this is due to choosing not to engage in such attempts when faced with the behavior, or because the opportunity simply did not arise.

Before turning to the results of our multivariate analyses, we first present bivariate analyses in order to establish the significance and directions of the relationships between analyzed variables. Table 5.3 presents a correlation matrix of the independent and dependent variables, along with sex and Greek membership (the only two demographic variables that were consistently correlated with

TABLE 5.3 Pearson correlation matrix of ordinal independent and dependent variables (p-values < .05 in bold)

	1	2	3	4	5	6	7	8	9	10	11	12
1. Adm. social control	—											
2. Success: Ad control	−.009	—										
3. Rec. social control	**.545**	−.062	—									
4. Success: Rec control	**.106**	**.404**	**−.214**	—								
5. Parental attachment	−.030	**.140**	**−.106**	**.240**	—							
6. School attachment	.069	**.104**	**−.183**	**.356**	**.224**	—						
7. Peer attachment	**.086**	**.188**	.055	**.278**	**.243**	**.166**	—					
8. Belief	−.071	**.176**	**−.216**	**.290**	**.190**	**.250**	**.121**	—				
9. Self-control	**−.156**	.010	**−.185**	−.018	.018	.029	.044	**.140**	—			
10. Peer deviance index	**.303**	**−.134**	**.325**	**−.205**	−.059	**−.165**	−.011	**−.408**	**−.163**	—		
11. R deviance index	**.188**	**−.105**	**.387**	**−.208**	**−.124**	**−.214**	.007	**−.496**	**−.249**	**.647**	—	
12. Male	−.033	**−.092**	−.010	−.079	−.036	**−.158**	**−.098**	**−.248**	−.053	**.182**	**.186**	—
13. Greek membership	**.212**	.047	**.122**	**.109**	**.080**	.006	**.106**	−.022	−.006	**.163**	**.151**	.005

our substantive variables). As we would expect, many of the control theory variables are positively related to each other and negatively related to deviance and peer deviance. For example, attachment to parents, school attachment, and peer attachment are all positively correlated with each other, and respondent deviance is negatively correlated with attachment to parents (–.124) and the school (–.214), and with belief in the law (–.496). These findings are consistent with Hirschi's (1969) findings and much of the previous research on social control theory. Contrary to Hirschi's findings (and Hypothesis 1), but consistent with some prior research, attachment to peers is not significantly correlated with peer or respondent deviance. The correlation between peer attachment and peer deviance (–.011), and between peer attachment and respondent deviance (.007) are both non-significant. In these data, at least, attachment to peers is not related to peer or respondent deviance. Self-control is negatively correlated with both peer deviance (–.163) and respondent deviance (–.249), and peer and respondent deviance are strongly correlated (.647).

Hypothesis 3 predicts that higher levels of social and self-control will be positively related to attempts at prosocial influence among peers and increase the likelihood that such attempts will be successful. The bivariate results suggest that these relationships are more complicated than what we predicted. The correlations between the independent and dependent variables suggest that social and self-control are correlated with attempts at informal social control, but not across all measures, or consistently in the predicted direction. With the exception of peer attachment, which was significant and positive, and self-control, which was significant and negative, the social control indexes were not correlated with administering control. Additionally, with the exception of peer attachment, those scoring higher on the measures of social/self-control are *less* likely to receive control, contrary to our predictions; but those with higher social control (but not self-control) are more likely to report that such efforts are successful, consistent with our predictions. Finally, consistent with the idea that social control attempts require opportunity (H4 and H5), both administering and receiving control are positively correlated with respondent and peer deviance.

Before proceeding to the multivariate analyses exploring the predictors of attempts at, and success of, prosocial peer influence, we present the results of preliminary analyses designed to evaluate whether our measures predict respondent deviance as we would expect based on past research. We expect that our measures of social and self-control will be negatively associated with deviance, and that peer deviance will be positively related to respondent deviance. Table 5.4 presents the results of our regressions of deviance on our demographic and independent variables. Model 1 is a baseline model that includes only the demographic control variables. Older students, males, and students who are members of a fraternity/sorority report significantly higher levels of deviance, while non-white students (compared to whites) self-report less deviance. Model 1 explains 7% of the variance in the deviance index. Model 2 adds our theoretical variables. Age, being white, and fraternity/sorority membership remain significant predictors of deviance, while sex becomes non-significant. Parental attachment is not a significant predictor of respondent deviance, unlike our findings in the bivariate analysis. School attachment, belief, and self-control are all negatively related to respondent deviance, so students who are more attached to school, who score higher on the belief scale, and who exhibit higher levels of self-control are less likely to report engaging in deviant behaviors. Peer attachment, however, is positively related to self-reported deviance, contrary to our predictions in Hypothesis 1, but consistent with some previous research. This model performs better explaining 34% of the variance in deviance as opposed to 7% explained variance in the first model.

TABLE 5.4 Ordinary least squares linear regression of respondent deviance (N = 686)

Variables	Models								
	1			*2*			*3*		
	b	*Beta*	P	b	*Beta*	P	b	*Beta*	P
Age	.296	.125	.001	.354	.150	.000	.205	.086	.002
Male	1.274	.164	.000	.255	.033	.311	−.023	−.003	.914
Non-white	−1.038	−.108	.005	−.884	−.088	.005	−.533	.053	.047
Frat/sorority	1.291	.141	.000	1.170	.128	.000	.467	.051	.058
Parental education	−.050	−.011	.771	.015	.003	.918	.013	.003	.916
Parental attachment				−.020	−.026	.446	−.028	−.037	.200
School attachment				−.075	−.093	.005	−.052	−.064	.022
Peer attachment				.186	.082	.012	.145	.064	.021
Belief				−.437	−.467	.000	−.264	−.282	.000
Self-control				−.562	−.143	.000	−.348	−.098	.000
Peer deviance							.511	.489	.000
Adjusted R²	.07			.34			.52		

Finally, Model 3 adds the peer deviance index to the predictor variables. Age and race remain significant, while Greek membership is no longer a significant predictor of deviance. The coefficients for school attachment, peer attachment, belief, and self-control remain significant. Belief (Beta = −0.282) and peer deviance (Beta = 0.489) are the strongest predictors in the model. The R^2 for Model 3 is 0.52, showing that our predictor variables are explaining a substantial portion of the variation in scores on the respondent deviance index.

We did not find much support for Hypothesis 1, which predicted that respondents who are more strongly attached to peers are less deviant and have fewer deviant peers than respondents who report weaker attachments to peers. The bivariate correlations between peer attachment and both respondent (r = 0.007) and peer deviance (r = −0.011) were not significant, and peer attachment is *positively* related to deviance in the regression models.[7] To determine which of the other variables in the model is producing this effect, we re-ran Model 3 from Table 5.4, omitting one independent variable at a time. When any of the other social control variables (belief, school attachment, or parental attachment) or self-control were dropped from the model, peer attachment was no longer a significant predictor of respondent deviance, suggesting that although the effect of attachment to peers on deviance is not moderated by peer deviance, it may be interacting with self-control and/ or one (or more) of the other measures of social control. We re-ran Model 3 a final time, to test for any interaction effects between peer attachment and self-control, parental attachment, school attachment, or belief. The effects of peer attachment did not differ across scores on the self-control, parental attachment, or school attachment indexes. The interaction term for peer attachment by belief, however, was significant and negative, suggesting that the positive effects of peer attachment on deviance are stronger when scores on the belief index are low then when scores on the belief index are high. Additional analyses not presented showed that scores on the deviance index decrease as peer attachment increases *for respondents who score high on the belief scale*. For those who score low on the belief scale, however, higher scores on peer attachment translate into higher scores on the deviance index. These findings are consistent with both social control and learning theories, in that people with a strong social bond on both of these indicators are less likely to be deviant, and people with a strong bond to friends but weak belief in the law are more likely to be deviant. The latter finding suggests that association with friends could be influencing attitudes in a pro-deviant direction. On the other hand, it is also possible that deviant behavior is causing a change in attitudes, a possibility that has received some empirical support (Minor 1984).

The findings from Table 5.4 are, for the most part, consistent with prior research, lending confidence to both our measures and to the adequacy of our sample to test our hypotheses about positive peer pressure.

Table 5.5 presents four regression models, predicting administering control (Model 1), administering control "success" (Model 2), receiving control (Model 3), and receiving control "success" (Model 4). These regressions provide tests of Hypotheses 2 through 5.

TABLE 5.5 OLS linear regression of administering social control, administering social control success, receiving control, and receiving control success

Variables	Models											
	1			*2*			*3*			*4*		
	AdmCntrl			*AC Success*			*RecCntrl*			*RC Success*		
	b	Beta	P	b	Beta	P	b	Beta	P	b	Beta	P
Age	−.078	−.019	.611	.031	.031	.444	−.035	−.012	.735	−.041	−.038	.363
Sex (male)	−.598	−.045	.233	−.148	−.045	.261	**−.959**	**−.100**	**.006**	.185	.052	.212
Race (non-white)	.923	.054	.139	.204	.048	.214	.733	.059	.090	.088	.020	.624
Greek membership (Yes)	**2.743**	**.173**	**.000**	.083	−.022	.574	.517	.046	.192	**.491**	**.121**	**.003**
Parental education	−.368	−.046	.209	−.046	−.024	.549	.236	.142	.242	−.089	−.042	.316
Parental attachment	−.079	−.060	.120	**.028**	**.085**	**.041**	−.057	−.061	.103	**.030**	**.085**	**.050**
School attachment	**.139**	**.100**	**.009**	.016	.044	.278	**−.146**	**−.145**	**.000**	**.101**	**.269**	**.000**
Peer attachment	.281	.072	.054	**.139**	**.141**	**.000**	**.261**	**.093**	**.010**	**.213**	**.189**	**.000**
Belief	.091	.056	.203	.036	.088	.058	.029	.025	.549	**.065**	**.151**	**.002**
Self-Control	**−.896**	**−.133**	**.000**	−.005	−.003	.938	**−.634**	**−.131**	**.000**	−.134	−.079	.051
Peer deviance	**.517**	**.288**	**.000**	−.039	−.088	.091	**.168**	**.130**	**.005**	**−.055**	**−.116**	**.033**
Respondent deviance	.015	.008	.869	.003	.008	.887	**.327**	**.265**	**.000**	−.009	−.021	.720
Adjusted R²	**.14**			**.06**			**.20**			**.23**		
N	686			643			632			484		

Hypothesis 2 predicts that higher levels of peer attachment will be positively related to attempts at prosocial influence among peers and increase the likelihood that such attempts will be successful. As seen in Model 1, peer attachment is not significantly related to administering control, but it is related to the success of administering control, as shown in Model 2. Models 3 and 4 show that, as predicted, respondents who are more strongly attached to their peers are more likely to receive positive peer influence, and to report that such influence attempts were successful. Consistent with the assumptions of social control theory, then, strong bonds between friends can translate into the willingness to attempt to positively influence peers, at least as reported by respondents experiencing control attempts from their friends. Also consistent with our predictions, those reporting stronger attachment to friends report more success at their attempts at positive peer pressure, and they report that their friends' attempts to influence them are also more successful.

Hypothesis 3 predicts that higher levels of social control and self-control will be positively related to attempts at prosocial influence among peers, and to the success of those attempts. Our analyses provide limited support for this hypothesis. Consistent with our expectations, respondents with stronger ties to school were more likely to administer control[8] (Model 1), and those with stronger ties to parents were more likely to perceive that attempts at administering control were successful (Model 2). Additionally, all of the social control variables were positively related to the success of received control attempts (Model 4). These findings are consistent with the idea that those more strongly tied to conventional institutions such as family and school, as well as those more tied to conventional beliefs, are more likely to attempt/experience positive peer influence, and to perceive that such attempts were successful.

Contrary to the predictions of Hypothesis 3, however, self-control was negatively related to both administering control (Model 1) and receiving control (Model 3). We assumed that higher self-control respondents would select themselves into non-deviant peer groups, and therefore would have fewer opportunities to engage in attempts at positive peer influence. But we also predicted that once we controlled for peer/respondent deviance, those with higher self-control would be more likely to report administering/receiving positive peer influence. Our analysis found the opposite, however. Controlling for peer/respondent deviance, those with high self-control are *less* likely to report administering or receiving control. One possible explanation for these seemingly contradictory findings is that having deviant peers and having the opportunity to attempt to positively influence deviant peers might not be synonymous. Perhaps non-deviant, high self-control respondents have some deviant friends, but unlike less conventional, low self-control respondents, select themselves out of the social *situations* where deviance is happening, thus giving them less opportunity to exert/receive informal social control.

To further explore this idea of conventional respondents with deviant friends, we performed simple cross-tabulation comparisons. We first created three categories of respondent and peer deviance—"none," "medium," and "high."[9] If we look at peer deviance scores for the 273 respondents who reported that they had not engaged in any of the deviant behaviors listed on the survey, not surprisingly, 44% reported that none of their peers had engaged in any of the deviant behaviors listed. What is interesting, however, is that 46% of the non-deviant respondents scored "medium" on the peer deviance index, while 10% scored "high." Clearly, even some of the most conventional of our respondents have deviant friends. We also looked at the 440 respondents who scored 16 on the self-control scale (range of 7–16, mean of 15). While 24% of these high self-control respondents indicated that their friends were "non-deviant," 36% of them scored "medium" on the peer deviance index, and 39% scored "high." These findings suggest that while peer and respondent deviance are highly correlated, we should be careful not to conflate the two. Because college life selects for more conventional young adults, the range of deviance is relatively narrow, and students may not select themselves into deviant or non-deviant friendship groups as clearly as they did in high school. The fact that many of our respondents are living in dorm rooms with assigned roommates and many nearby neighbors might also play a role—roommates and neighbors cannot be as freely chosen as can other friends, particularly for first-year students. This might contribute to the possibility that more conventional students with higher levels of self-control have deviant friends but select themselves out of deviant situations. It would be interesting for future research to take advantage of the natural experiment provided by assigned roommates among first-year college students in order to study peer influence on deviance and conformity.

Hypotheses 4 and 5 are derived from the opportunity perspective and predict that the more deviant the respondents' friends, the more likely respondents are to try to control their friends' behavior, independent of levels of social and self-control; and the more deviant the respondents, the more likely they are to report receiving control from their peers, independent of their levels of social and self-control. We found strong support for both of these predictions. Respondents with more deviant peers are more likely to have attempted to influence them positively (Model 1), and more deviant respondents are, in turn, more likely to receive social control from their peers (Model 3). This is consistent with the idea that membership in deviant peer groups creates opportunities to engage in attempts at prosocial influence, and that even deviant respondents recognize that there are some situations in which deviance should be discouraged and prosocial behavior encouraged.

The standardized coefficients for deviance and peer deviance show that the best predictors in our models of administering control (Model 1) and receiving control (Model 3) are opportunity effects—those with the most deviant peers are the most likely to try to influence their behavior positively, and the most deviant respondents are most likely to have friends try to influence their behavior positively. The various social control measures are more consistently related to the *success* of attempts at social control (Models 2 and 4) than they are to the frequency of the attempts themselves (Models 1 and 3).

When comparing the importance of social control and self-control vs. opportunity variables, it is clear from our analyses that both sets of theoretical constructs exert independent effects on peer informal social control. To provide a more visual (and intuitive) summary of the findings, utilizing a method employed by Soss, Langbein, and Metalko (2003), Figures 5.1 through 5.4 provide graphical displays of the relative effects of the significant predictor variables based on the regression models presented in Table 5.5. The estimates displayed in the figures show the maximum impact of each predictor variable on the predicted value of the outcome variable(s), computed by setting all the other variables in the regression model to their means and shifting each independent variable from its observed minimum to its observed maximum. By presenting the effects of each significant coefficient graphically, we can see how much the predicted value of each outcome variable changes over the range of scores for each independent variable. For instance, in Figure 5.1, which graphically displays the significant coefficients from the regression for administering control, Greek membership increases the predicted score on the administering control scale by 2.74 points. The difference between the predicted score on the administering control scale when school attachment is at its lowest value versus its highest value is 3.6. Self-control exerts the largest impact—the difference in the predicted value of the administering control scale is 8.06 points higher when self-control is lowest than when self-control is highest. Finally, the difference in the predicted value of the administering control scale is 6.2 points higher when peer deviance is at its highest score than when it is at its lowest score. Figure 5.2 presents the significant coefficients for receiving control, showing the maximum estimated impact of sex, school attachment, peer attachment, self-control, and peer and respondent deviance. The graphs in Figures 5.1 and 5.2 are scaled the same, since the range in the two outcome variables are similar (13–49 for administering control, and 12–46 for receiving control). Figures 5.3 and 5.4 present graphic displays of the significant coefficients for administering control success and receiving control success (since both variables have a range of 2–10, they are scaled the same).

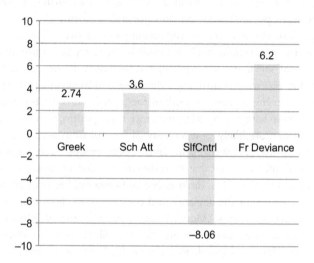

FIGURE 5.1 Maximum estimated impact on administering control (range 13–49, mean = 25.52)

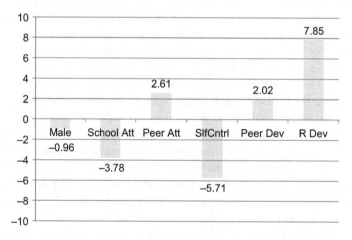

FIGURE 5.2 Maximum estimated impact on receiving control (range 12–46, mean = 18.16)

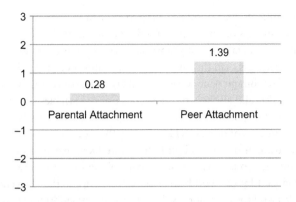

FIGURE 5.3 Maximum estimated impact on administering control success (range 2–10, mean = 6.65)

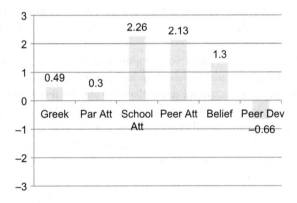

FIGURE 5.4 Maximum estimated impact on receiving control success (range 2–10, mean = 7.25)

Discussion and Conclusions

It is clear that criminologists have been missing much of interest by only focusing on peers as a source of *deviant* influence. Our results show that positive peer influence is common, and that peers try to keep each other from engaging in a wide range of deviant behaviors and encourage each other toward positive and productive behavior. Their attempts are often successful, which means that the respondents in our sample have prevented hundreds, if not thousands, of deviant acts.

Based on predictions derived from social control theory and self-control theory, we expected that those with higher levels of attachment to peers, higher levels of the social bond in general, and higher levels of self-control would be more concerned with the welfare of their friends and thus more likely to attempt to influence their behavior positively. Our hypotheses received mixed support. Peer attachment was positively related to being the target of prosocial influence attempts, but was not related to respondents' likelihood of trying to control their peers' behavior. It was, however, positively related to the success of both types of influence attempts, consistent with our predictions.

Our other measures of social control theory constructs were more consistently related to the "success" of influence attempts than they were of the attempts themselves. Respondents who scored higher on the parental attachment scale were more likely to report that their attempts at administering control were successful, and all three of the social control variables (parental attachment, school attachment, and belief) were positively related to the success of received control attempts. It seems that sensitivity to the opinions of others, as Hirschi (1969) put it, is a very apt description of a strong bond to society. The stronger our social bonds, the more likely we are to be influenced by others' direct attempts at controlling our behavior. Social control theory has focused largely on indirect and internal controls produced by our bonds to society, for example the "psychological presence" of parents (Hirschi 1969: 88). However, our results suggest that when indirect controls fail, those with a stronger social bond are more likely to be affected by direct controls exerted by peers. As Cullen put it, "social support often is a precondition for effective social control" (1994: 545). Our results are also consistent with Sampson and Laub's (1993) finding that men with strong bonds to their wives are more likely to desist from crime, at least in part as a result of wives' direct controls over their behavior (see also Laub and Sampson 2003). Our data do not allow us to determine whether this effect would hold for influence toward deviant behavior as well. This will be an important question for future research to address.

Interestingly, and contrary to our predictions, respondents with higher levels of self-control were less likely to try to control their friends' behavior, or to report that their friends attempted to control their behavior. As discussed above, we speculate that this may be due to the fact that those with higher self-control may be less likely to be in the presence of their deviant peers while their friends are engaging in deviant behavior. In other words, they may have deviant friends, but they might also be more likely to decline their friends' invitations to join them in their deviant or potentially deviant behavior. For example, if a friend invites another friend to a party, and the friend declines the invitation, that friend is unlikely to be able to keep the first friend from drinking and driving at the end of the night. In this sense, controlling for friends' deviance may not be sufficient to control for opportunity to exert positive peer influence—one may have friends or roommates who like to party a lot, but at the same time not join them in their partying.[10] This distinction between situational influence and more general influence processes is an important one that future research might try to address.

Finally, some of the clearest and most interesting findings from our analyses are those relating to the impact that deviance and peer deviance had on our measures of peer informal social control. Conventional wisdom might lead one to predict that deviant peers exert primarily "deviant" influence over one another, and that conventional peers exert primarily "conventional" influence over one another. Our results, however, show that respondents with more deviant friends were actually most likely to both administer and receive social control—consistent with Hypotheses 4 and 5. The relative effect sizes of our independent variables clearly show that the best predictor of trying to control one's friends' behavior is their level of deviance, and the best predictor of friends trying to control the individual's behavior is the individual's level of deviance. These results are very consistent with opportunity-based theories such as routine activities theory (Cohen and Felson 1979; Osgood and Anderson 2004). Although opportunity theories have not been applied to the explanation of positive peer pressure, their logic is essentially that easy opportunity is an excellent predictor of what people are likely to do. Having deviant friends presents the opportunity to exert pressure toward non-deviant behavior.

On the other hand, these results are very damaging to aspects of cultural deviance and learning theories of crime and delinquency—especially those suggesting that members of deviant peer groups "socialize" one another to non-normative values, or consistently encourage/reward deviant behavior. Although we saw in Chapter 3 that peers can have a negative influence on each other's behavior, our results in this chapter show that the most deviant respondents in the data set experience the greatest attempts at peer social control toward conformity. Similarly, the respondents with the most deviant friends are most likely to try to reduce their friends' deviance. This is true despite the fact that friends' deviance is strongly associated with the individual's deviance, consistent with prior research. The picture this paints of deviant friendship groups is that there are groups of friends engaging in deviant behavior together, but at the same time recognizing the potential harm that can result from that behavior and trying to keep each other out of harm's way. Clearly, then, these data do not support a norm transference explanation of deviant behavior, with groups of friends rewarding and encouraging deviant attitudes. Rather, the data are much more consistent with the control theory assumption of social order, that even those who engage in deviant behavior know it's wrong. Members of peer groups may come together to engage in enjoyable, exciting, and deviant behavior, despite the fact that they know the behavior can have potentially damaging physical, social, and legal consequences.

Finally, we also have evidence of traditional selection effects from our respondents' comments at the end of the survey. The most common response to an open-ended question asking for any final comments about the survey was from respondents who wrote to explain their lack of experience with positive peer influence. Most wrote that when they answered "never" to the questions about whether they had administered or received social control, it was not because deviant behaviors were occurring and they or their friends chose not to attempt to exert positive influence, but because such behaviors *simply did not occur*. For example:

> Many of the questions in this survey do not apply to the social group with which I normally interact. None of my closest friends ever use drugs in my presence if at all and are all very future-oriented. The wildest we ever got was taking multiple 5-hour Energies one time, and we all agreed the next day never to do that again.

> There should have been a "N/A" option for the questions in which you asked whether or not I influenced my friends in a particular way. None of the close friends I have are involved in the drinking or partying scene, so there is never a need for me to convince them not to drive drunk, etc.

> I would like to note that the reason that I have not tried to discourage my friends from doing risky things, or that my friends have not tried to prevent me from doing the same is because we don't really do risky things. I know a lot of people say that, but we don't. We haven't had to discourage each other because the situation never arose, but if it did happen, I'm sure that we would stand up for each other. I really hope that you all are taking factors like this into consideration for your study. Sometimes people don't act because there is no reason to.

> Please remember that some people, myself included, might have stated that they didn't interfere with a friend making bad choices simply because their friends weren't making those bad choices in the first place, thus there was no need to step in. Which is a good thing. =)

I hope it's ok that none of my friends smoke or drink or party. Mostly, we just eat cake and watch movies. Or talk. Lots of talking. And homework.

Some of the initial questions didn't seem to explicitly state a proper meaning. For instance, "Have you tried to encourage a friend to wear a seat-belt in the past year?" All my friends realize the importance of the seat-belt so I don't need to remind them, so I answered never. However, simply answering "never" can also imply that I simply don't care about my friend's safety and didn't remind him of the seat-belt's marvelous safety features.

These respondents clearly point out the importance of opportunity for positive peer pressure, and also provide some useful suggestions for future research. Some of them were clearly bothered by the idea that their failure to intervene in friends' deviance might appear to be a matter of choice rather than opportunity, which is an interesting finding in its own right.

Notes

1. Unless otherwise noted, we used the same process to create all of the additive indexes in the regression models. We first entered the items into a principle component analysis with Varimax rotation. In all cases, the analysis either produced a one-factor solution, or produced a multi-factor solution where there was a significant gap between the first and subsequent eigenvalues, suggesting a one-factor solution. Finally, Tabachnick and Fidell (2007) suggest 0.45 as a cutoff for factor loading scores, so items with loading scores below 0.45 were dropped.
2. Seventy percent of the sample has scores on the Receiving Control Success, 91% on the Administering Control Success.
3. We initially created two self-control scales—one attitudinal and one behavioral. The attitudinal index did not predict deviance or three of our four substantive dependent variables, so we dropped the attitudinal measures of self-control from the analyses.
4. Although the behavioral self-control scale ranges from 7–16, the mean of 15.33 obviously indicates that the majority of the sample answered "never" to the four individual items, and that there is very little variation in the distribution of scores. In hindsight, it would have been more appropriate to preface these questions with "have you ever" rather than "in the last year."
5. We initially ran the analyses with dummy variables for all the non-white racial/ethnic categories (Black, Asian, Hispanic, Native American, and Other), but they did not end up being significant predictors in the final models of any of the analyses. For the sake of parsimony, we ran the regressions using a single dichotomous race variable, "Non-white," assigning the 18% of students who answered no to the yes/no "White" racial identification question a score of 1.
6. Sample self-selection effects may also explain this finding—i.e., those most likely to take the time to voluntarily fill out a survey are likely more conventional than those who do not, and therefore may be "administering" more social control than they are "receiving."
7. We also re-ran Model 3 with the addition of an interaction term to determine if the effects of peer attachment differed by scores on the peer deviance index. The interaction term was not significant, however, suggesting that regardless of the deviance of one's peers, higher scores on the peer attachment index are related to higher scores on the deviance index. This finding is counter to predictions made by both social learning and social control theories.
8. Interestingly, while respondents who are more strongly attached to school report more frequent attempts at positively influencing their friends (Model 1), they report fewer incidents where friends attempted to influence them (Model 3). Recall that both the administering and receiving control indexes include a question asking about encouraging a friend (or receiving encouragement from a friend) to "work harder at school." It seems likely that better students are more likely to encourage their friends to follow their example and work hard at school than they are to receive such encouragement from their friends.
9. For the respondent deviance index, which ranged from 0 to 24 with a mean of 2.86, we coded the 36% of the sample who reported engaging in none of the deviant acts listed on the survey as "none." The 39% of

the sample scoring between 1 and 4 on the deviance index were coded as "medium," and the 24% who scored between 4 and 24 were coded as "high." For the peer deviance index (which ranged from 0 to 12 with a mean of 4.04), we coded the 23% of the sample who reported that none of their peers had engaged in any of the listed behaviors as "none," the 35% who scored between 1 and 4 on the peer deviance index were coded as "medium," while the 40% who scored between 5 and 12 were coded as "high."

10. Another alternative explanation for this finding is that individuals with high self-control view attempts at exerting control as potentially risky behaviors, so if they are in a situation where friends are engaging in deviance, they choose not to interfere. Additionally, if they themselves are unlikely to engage in deviance, then others are unlikely to attempt to exert control over them.

6

CONCLUSIONS AND RECOMMENDATIONS FOR FUTURE RESEARCH AND POLICY

It is clear from our analyses that the field of criminology has missed a great deal in its understanding of peer influence. We have relied too much on the use of quantitative methods that, by their very nature, are ill-suited to tapping into the peer influence process. For the most part, criminologists have focused on improving quantitative research design and analytical methods, and we have forgotten to ask more basic questions, such as the ones motivating this research—exactly what is happening in the context of peer interactions that can lead toward or away from deviant or dangerous behavior? As Laub and Sampson put it, ". . . the development of quantitative methods has solidified criminology's claim as a scientific enterprise, but what criminology is lacking is a rich, detailed knowledge base about offending from those who commit crime, expressed in their own words" (2003: 59).

It is also clear that criminologists have missed a great deal by only focusing on the questions of how and to what extent peers influence each other's criminal or deviant behavior. We should have also been asking how and to what extent peers keep each other out of trouble and motivate each other toward positive, productive, and prosocial behaviors. The early research that guided inquiry into the "peer effect" is probably responsible for this focus. As we noted at the outset, the idea that bad companions can have a negative effect on one's behavior is thousands of years old, and it was a fundamental idea behind some of the earliest and most influential works in criminology, including Shaw and McKay's (1942) work on delinquency in Chicago, Sutherland's (1947) differential association theory, Miller's (1958) conception of a lower-class culture as a cause of delinquency, and even some variations of strain theory that included discussions of the role of criminal or delinquent subcultures in promoting deviance in strained individuals (Cloward and Ohlin 1960; Cohen 1955).

Because of the emphasis on culture and learning deviant norms as a cause of delinquency, later theorists who disagreed with this view focused on refuting it. For example, Hirschi (1969) focused on testing hypotheses derived from cultural explanations of delinquency against the Gluecks's contention that "birds of a feather flock together" (Glueck and Glueck 1950; cited in Hirschi 1969: 136). Consistent the with Gluecks's conclusions, Hirschi's evidence led him to conclude that a weakened social bond preceded both association with delinquent peers and delinquent behavior. By focusing on disproving the cultural deviance argument, Hirschi may have overlooked the possibility that peers can have a direct causal influence on conformity, which is a possibility that is quite consistent with his theory.

Similarly, Kornhauser's (1978) evaluation of the major competing theories of crime focused explicitly on the incompatibility of the fundamental assumptions of cultural deviance theories and control theories. Cultural deviance theories like Sutherland's, she argued, assume that group values can vary without limit. Kornhauser argued that the theory must make this assumption given its argument that adherence to group values cause crimes such theft and murder, which are clearly antithetical to the functioning of social groups. Cultural theories also must assume that human nature is good or prosocial, in that individuals will not commit crime unless they have been taught values that support it (Kornhauser 1978). In contrast, Kornhauser argued that control theories make essentially opposite assumptions. Human nature is asocial or selfish, which allows for the possibility that individuals can violate the norms of their own group. Given this view of human nature, in order for societies to exist, there must be some basic agreement on fundamental rules of behavior and some method of enforcing them (Kornhauser 1978).

Kornhauser's analysis of the logic and empirical evidence in support of these contrasting theories led to her resounding rejection of cultural deviance models. It was perhaps the forcefulness of her rejection that furthered theoretical debate between control theorists and cultural deviance theorists. Subsequent empirical analyses continued to focus on the same basic predictions that had been tested for years, albeit with increasing methodological sophistication (e.g., Costello and Vowell 1999; Matsueda 1982). The theoretical debate continued as well (e.g., Akers 1996; Costello 1997; Hirschi 1996), and a number of "integrated theories" attempted to resolve these debates by combining elements of learning theories and control theories (e.g., Elliott, Huizinga, and Ageton 1985).

More recent research has moved to the use of network analysis to determine the characteristics of groups that seem to increase the level of deviance of their members (e.g., Haynie 2001). The basic issue, however, has remained the same—do delinquent peers cause delinquency, as learning theories argue, or is the observed correlation largely or entirely spurious, consistent with control theories? Again, we believe that the focus on only these two possibilities has led criminologists to overlook the idea that peers, even delinquent peers, might provide direct social control on each other's behavior and influence each other toward conformity.

Key Findings

Negative Peer Influence

Our unique approach in this work has led to several important findings. First, there is a great deal of situational peer pressure toward deviance, despite the fact that most criminological literature has dismissed this possibility (Akers 1998; Gottfredson and Hirschi 1990; Warr 2002). Our research uncovered a variety of mechanisms of negative influence that seem to fit the category of "peer pressure," including coercive tactics such as ridicule, trying to convince a friend to deviate by minimizing the potential negative consequences of the behavior, and inducing deviance in others for the amusement of onlookers. Including these types of influence, along with "deviance loves company" and "fear of loss of status," a total of 108 incidents classified into specific categories seem to fit the conception of peer pressure, or 57% of all classified incidents in our data set. This suggests that we need to pay much more attention to the influence of "short-term, situationally-induced" motives for deviance in addition to enduring characteristics of individuals like values, social bonds, and levels of self-control (Briar and Piliavin 1965: 36).

We also found evidence that youths believe that participating in deviance, such as drinking or drug use, will make them more likeable to those who engage in such behaviors, regardless of whether it's actually true. This finding is consistent with literature on deviance and substance use that discusses "shared misunderstandings" (Warr 2002), false consciousness and projection (Boman et al. 2012; Prinstein and Wang 2005), or "perceived norms" (Perkins, Haines, and Rice 2005) as causes of participation in deviance. It is also consistent with research showing higher rates of delinquency among adolescents who worry about social approval (Young and Weerman 2013), as well as research finding that fear of ridicule or ostracism might motivate conformity even when actual ridicule has not been experienced or threatened (Lashbrook 2000). Scheff's (1990) analysis of the famous Asch (1956) experiments notes this process, in that the subjects who conformed to a clearly inaccurate group opinion perceived the potential for ostracism, although the group made no overt threat to that effect (Lashbrook 2000). In our results, these kinds of perceptions were more often reported by respondents in our 2009 sample, many of whom were describing initiation into drug or alcohol use in the years before they entered college. It would be interesting for future research to examine the frequency with which these processes operate among youth of various ages, as it seems likely that they are more common among younger people.

Finally, there was substantial evidence of a simple opportunity effect, with a total of 69 references to "simple offers or invitations" to deviance, or 36% of incidents described. This possibility is most often suggested by control theorists and routine activities theorists (Gottfredson and Hirschi 1990; Hirschi 1969; Osgood and Anderson 2004), and is most consistent with the argument that self-selection explains the correlation between delinquency and peer delinquency. Based on our data, it's common that individuals who enjoy engaging in the same deviant behaviors tend to associate with each other, as the self-selection argument would hold. It is also common that individual incidents of deviant behavior are induced by invitations from others. Thus, our data show that both self-selection and peer influence via simple invitations contribute to an individual's overall incidence of deviance.

Perhaps the most interesting finding in our analysis of the negative peer influence data lies in what we did not find. There is very little evidence in our data of processes that are consistent with differential association or learning theories (Burgess and Akers 1966; Sutherland 1947). The focus in these theories is on deviant peers teaching norms or values that are conducive to deviance, and the reinforcement of behaviors that reflect those norms and values. While we did find that respondents' expectations or perceptions of others' norms or values motivated their participation in deviant behavior in some cases, we found almost no evidence in those cases that deviant peers did anything more than model deviant behavior. Only two respondents even mentioned moral issues surrounding deviance in their accounts of negative peer influence, and one of them was critical of the failure of others to react to a behavior that he or she thought was morally wrong.

Further, even the types of influence that seem to exemplify the concept of "peer pressure" do not seem consistent with the norm-transference explanations offered by learning theories. We discussed previously the idea that much of the negative influence we saw in our data seemed motivated by selfish concerns, such as the desire to be entertained by the dangerous antics of intoxicated friends. Other instances of peer pressure seemed motivated by a desire to diffuse responsibility for a behavior that the respondent him- or herself perhaps thought was unacceptable, such as the respondent who convinced an 11-year-old to smoke marijuana with him or her to avoid feeling like a "stoner" by smoking alone. In other cases, it's not clear why individuals pressured each other to engage in deviance, such as the fraternity brothers who broke into another brother's room and demanded he drink alcohol while he was writing a paper, and left him alone after he took a couple of drinks.

In any case, the emphasis in learning theories on learning "an excess of definitions favorable to violation of law over definitions unfavorable to violation of law" (Sutherland, Cressey, and Luckenbill 1992: 89) is entirely unsupported by our data. As we noted previously, limitations in our sample preclude us from making conclusions about any larger group, and because we measure only situational types of influence we cannot make any general conclusions about peer influence that might occur over time. That having been said, the lack of evidence in our data for norm transference processes is striking.

On the basis of these results, we agree with other scholars' claims that norm transference holds little value as an explanation of the peer effect (Warr 2002). Thus, we argue that traditional cultural and social learning explanations of crime and deviance hold little value in explaining peer influence processes. Alternative conceptualizations of culture might hold more promise in explaining peer influence on deviance (Kirk and Papachristos 2011; Sampson and Bartusch 1998; Sampson and Bean 2006; Swidler 1986). For example, Swidler (1986) is critical of the traditional view of culture as "end-values" that shape or determine behavior, and argues that culture is better viewed as a toolkit from which actions are selected. People tend to stick with familiar strategies of action, habits, or ways of doing things, even when it might be to their benefit to do things differently. Sampson and Bean (2006) ague that culture is also performative and relational, "embodied practices as played out on a public stage, not beliefs encased in the individual mind" (Sampson and Bean 2006: 30). This view of culture as emerging from social interaction holds much more promise in understanding the processes of situational peer influence we observed in our data than does the more traditional approach of differential association and social learning theories. It may be that going along with what one's peers are doing is habitual, and it might also be standard behavior to convince one's friends to go along with one's behavior even if they don't seem to want to. This view might help explain the similarities we found in methods of positive and negative peer influence, and also implies that research should focus on general processes of peer influence rather than only on peer influence toward deviance.

Positive Peer Influence

Despite the almost complete lack of attention in the criminological literature to positive peer influence processes, our second major finding in this work is that positive influence is very common. Our respondents reported more incidents of positive peer influence than negative in our qualitative data, and our quantitative analyses showed that a large majority of our respondents report incidents of trying to influence their friends' behavior either away from deviance or toward positive or prosocial behaviors such as exercising more, working harder at school, and so on. Sixty-seven percent of our respondents reported trying to prevent friends from drinking and driving, and about 86% of respondents reported trying to get friends to work harder at school. The number of students reporting being the recipient of attempts at social control from their friends was lower, but still substantial—about 23% of students reported others trying to prevent them from drinking and driving, and about 65% of respondents reported their friends encouraging them to work harder at school.

Our qualitative results show some similarities in the mechanisms peers use to try to influence behavior positively and negatively. Simple opportunity effects were evident in a total of 20% of incidents that were assigned to one of the specific categories of positive influence. These incidents often took the form of offering to give an intoxicated friend a ride home, or a respondent issuing an invitation for a friend to exercise or study with him or her. These incidents demonstrated that it was often quite easy for friends to steer each other away from deviance. It wasn't always that easy, however—coercive tactics were quite common, with 36% of all classified incidents fitting this category. A typical incident of coercion might involve an intoxicated person refusing a simple offer of a ride home, which led friends to resort to physical force or trickery to get the person's keys away from him or her. Threats to end a relationship as a result of poor behavior were also fairly common.

We found one major difference between types of coercion used in positive versus negative influence attempts, with ridicule being fairly common for negative influence but virtually absent for positive influence. This may be the result of differing motives for influence attempts. If one's motives are more altruistic, one may be less likely to use a potentially ostracizing method of influence such as ridicule. On the other hand, if one is motivated to influence another's behavior for one's own benefit, the relative lack of concern for the other might take the form of ridicule. We did not explicitly ask our respondents to report their motives for peer influence, and we think it will be important for future research to do so.

Another difference between positive and negative influence techniques was in the frequency with which respondents emphasized the consequences of a behavior. This type of influence was used in a total of 30% of positive influence descriptions and 15% of cases of negative influence. Examples of positive influence include someone emphasizing the negative effects of smoking or drug use to get a friend to change his or her behavior or emphasizing the potential positive effects of exercising more. Typically, when influencing a friend toward deviant behavior, the potential for getting into trouble or the potential for physical harm was minimized. Again, this might be the result of differences in motives—if one's interest is in gathering a group of friends to drink or use drugs with, telling friends that drugs are "all natural" and not bad for them, as one of our respondents did, makes sense. On the other hand, if one is genuinely concerned for one's friends' health, pointing out the potential health risks of the behavior might be an effective influence technique.

Trying to influence a friend for the benefit or entertainment of others was a much less common technique of positive influence (less than 2%) than negative influence (about 13%). Apparently, it's more fun to watch one's friends doing deviant or dangerous things than it is to watch them engage in conforming behavior. The existence of television shows like *Jackass*, and the prevalence of YouTube videos featuring the antics of drunken people jumping off roofs would appear to bear this out. These results are consistent with our speculation that positive influence attempts may be more altruistically motivated and negative influence might be more self-interested. Encouraging a friend to do something for one's own entertainment that could cause serious harm seems pretty selfish. As one of our respondents noted, "What sorts of friends treat each other in this manner?"

Finally, there were more appeals to morality among the positive influence descriptions than there were for negative influence, with 10 of our respondents pointing out the immorality of behaviors to try to steer their friends away from them. This is still a surprisingly small number given our sample size, and this supports our conclusions that norms, values, or moral standards are not often invoked as a method of influencing peers' behavior, at least in our sample.

The results of our quantitative analyses revealed some interesting patterns. The clearest results in all of our analyses were the findings indicating that opportunity is the most important determinant of attempts at positive peer influence. Positive influence is most common when one's peers are most deviant, and receiving positive peer influence attempts is more likely when the individual is most deviant. Our control theory measures did not predict positive influence attempts very well; contrary to our expectation that those with a stronger bond to their friends, and to society in general, and those with higher self-control would be more likely to attempt to use positive peer pressure. However, given the strong correlation in our data between individual and peer deviance, our data show that even deviant individuals attempt to steer their friends toward conformity. This finding is supportive of control theory's assumption of the existence of a single moral order (Hirschi 1969; Gottfredson and Hirschi 1990). Even those who engage in deviant or dangerous behavior recognize that such behavior may not be the best idea, and at least at some level they seem to recognize the potential negative consequences of that behavior (Warr 2002). Again, then, we find little evidence to suggest general acceptance of deviance, even among those who engage in it themselves. This finding is very difficult to reconcile with theories that focus on learning processes, deviant norms, or moral values as key causes of crime. It is interesting to consider the parallels between our micro-level findings and those from macro-level studies showing little tolerance for deviance among those in high-crime communities (e.g., Sampson and Bartusch 1998). The university campus might be viewed as a high-deviance social environment, at least among some groups of students. At the same time, attempts at controlling deviance are also high, perhaps indicating a lack of normative acceptance of deviance even among those who engage in it.

Our predictions regarding the success of influence attempts were better supported—those reporting greater attachment to friends reported greater success of positive influence attempts, both those they administered and those they received, consistent with social control theory. This is an important finding, because for practical purposes, it doesn't matter much whether friends try to influence each other's behavior if those influence attempts are not successful. If we try to develop crime-prevention programs that encourage peer or bystander intervention in imminent crimes, it would be very useful to know the circumstances under which intervention might be more successful. Our results suggest that such attempts are likely be more successful among those with stronger bonds to society in general and to their friends in particular.

Limitations and Implications for Further Research and Policy

Our study has some important limitations, first among them being the lack of representativeness of our sample and the relatively conforming nature of college students. Although there is no lack of deviant behavior among college students, their rate of participation in serious crimes is fairly low. It is not safe to generalize from our data to peer influence processes that might be involved in more serious crimes. In all of our data, there were only a few references to any violent crimes or potential instances of sexual assault, for example, and few references to property crimes of any significance. It is possible that the lack of reference to moral values in our data reflects the relatively non-serious nature of much of the deviance engaged in by our respondents. Although drinking and driving is a serious crime that can result in death, it is probably safe to say that most cases of drinking and driving do not result in accident or injury, and most of the behaviors our respondents engaged in were victimless offenses. Thus, the extent to which the mechanisms of peer influence we uncovered are used by more serious offenders is not known. Future researchers would be well-advised to study these processes among younger children, particularly those who are at the typical age of initiation into deviant behaviors such as drug and alcohol use. It would also be useful to study these processes among gang members and other youth living in high-crime areas.

One of the major strengths of our work, our focus on exactly what happens in situations involving peer influence, is also one of its limitations. Because we focus only on situational influences, we have not attempted to tap into peer influence processes that might occur over a longer period of time in the course of a friendship. This is potentially an important limitation in light of our claim that learned values do not appear to be an important mechanism of peer influence. To the extent that one's friends can impact norms and values, this influence is likely to occur over time rather than in a single situation. On the other hand, we did see accounts of initiation into new deviant behaviors, and even in these cases there was generally no discussion of moral concerns about the behaviors. In any case, it might be useful for future researchers to collect qualitative, longitudinal research data that can measure both friendship processes that occur over time and interactional processes that occur in particular situations. Existing longitudinal studies in criminology focusing on peer influence have been based only on quantitative data that do not measure learning or influence processes—these designs are clearly inadequate to measure the mechanisms of peer influence, and have only furthered the questionable notion that increased similarity over time in friends' behavior supports normative or learning explanations of peer influence (e.g., Haynie 2001; Matsueda and Anderson 1998).

Policy Considerations

Current efforts to reduce deviant behavior among college students often consist of educational programs that are designed to change behavior through changing norms. There is a great deal of evidence suggesting that this approach does not work. For example, most efforts at reducing binge drinking among college students have been educational programs and efforts to change perceptions of drinking norms on campus (Wechsler et al. 2002). These programs have had little effect on rates of binge drinking over time (Wechsler et al. 2002). Similarly, programs designed to debunk "rape myths" and other educational programs have failed to reduce rates of campus rape over time (Armstrong, Hamilton, and Sweeney 2006). Journalist Tina Rosenberg argues convincingly that educational programs designed to reduce behaviors such as smoking and risky sexual behavior among teens have not worked, and she instead advocates systematic attempts to encourage positive peer pressure to reduce these behaviors (2011).

We believe that the purely educational approach to preventing crime and deviance has failed to solve problems largely because everyone knows that behaviors like binge drinking, smoking, rape, and other forms of deviant or criminal behavior are wrong or potentially harmful in some way. As Warr (2002) notes, offenders recognize that their crimes might result in legal consequences, and virtually everyone who has ever had too much to drink is aware of the physical consequences that might occur immediately, like getting sick, or the consequences that arrive the following morning in the form of a hangover. If knowledge, norms, or values were key to changing people's behavior, we wouldn't see two-thirds of American adults overweight or obese.

We have presented evidence that suggests that we pay more attention to peer influence as both a cause of and a deterrent to deviance among college students. There is evidence that these processes may be at work in much more serious behavior than what we have studied. For example, there is evidence friendship ties are a more important motivator than ideology in joining jihadist organizations (Sageman 2004). Some reports suggest that ISIS recruits western converts primarily through establishing friendship ties, and only secondarily by indoctrinating recruits into radical ideology. "Alex," a 23-year-old American woman, began chatting online with an ISIS recruiter "for hours every day, their interactions giddy, filled with smiley faces and exclamations of 'LOL'" (Callimachi 2015). Despite the innocuous beginning, Alex eventually made plans to travel abroad and meet her recruiter and a potential husband. In this case, the recruiter was clearly trying to create an attachment and then exploit that bond to lure Alex into ISIS. Although there are obvious differences between this situation and those reported in our data, this recruitment attempt seems to be consistent with a selfishly-motivated "peer" trying to use loyalty to involve someone else in potentially deviant behavior. Thus, the study of how peer influence works in more ordinary situations might help us understand how to better counter this influence in more serious cases.

There is some research suggesting that enlisting peers to reduce bullying may be an effective tactic. Evidence is equivocal, however, and suggests that interventions targeting peers as agents of social control might only be effective among younger children (Salmivalli, Kaukiainen, and Voeten 2005). We believe that learning more about when and under what circumstances kids do intervene might be an important first step in creating programs to reduce bullying. It might be useful to ask children direct questions about situations in which they've intervened in bullying, or failed to intervene, and their explanations of why they did or did not do so.

Our line of research might be similarly applicable to programs on college campuses designed to enlist peers to reduce rates of sexual assault. One such program, Mentors in Violence Prevention (MVP), is designed to foster bystander intervention in situations of violence against women in particular (Katz 2015). The focus in this program is on training both men and women to intervene by presenting them with scenarios and discussing possible reactions to those situations. Other programs with a similar approach are the Men's Program, which attempts to prevent rape through a "powerful male-on-male victim empathy component" and training to encourage bystander intervention (Langhinrichsen-Rohling et al. 2011: 745); and Banyard, Moynihan, and Plante's (2007) Bringing in the Bystander Program. While there is evidence that these programs can change attitudes among college students, it is not clear that they have had any effect on actual rates of sexual assault (Banyard, Plante, and Moynihan 2004; Cissner 2009; Langhinrichsen-Rohling et al. 2011). For example, evaluations show increases in respondents' reported efficacy, or the extent to which they feel that they could intervene in instances of possible sexual assault (Banyard et al. 2004; Langhinrichsen-Rohling et al. 2011), but the effects of these programs on actual behavior have not been determined. In light of our findings, we suggest that it would also be useful to learn more about the situations in which people have intervened to prevent sexual assault in the "real world," and then develop programs that might foster similar behavior among others, or suggest ways to structure social situations to reduce opportunity for such offenses.

We hope our work will spur a new research agenda in the field of criminology, one that recognizes the potentially powerful impact of positive peer pressure, and one that continues to focus on mechanisms of negative peer influence other than learned norms and values. We believe that efforts at crime and delinquency prevention could benefit from such research, as basic research on positive influence strategies that are effective could lead to prevention efforts that are more likely to be successful than what we've tried in the past. A broader approach to the study of peer influence processes will also further our understanding of the causes of both crime and conformity.

APPENDIX A

Paper Assignment for URI 2009 Sample

Sociology 100, General Sociology
Fall 2009
Extra Credit Paper Assignment—Due Wednesday, October 28 at the beginning of class

This is a request for your assistance with an area of research that is of particular interest to me, which is peer influence toward both "positive" and "negative" behavior. My area of specialization in sociology is crime and delinquency, and one of the most robust findings in the delinquency literature is that kids who engage in delinquent or criminal behavior tend to have friends who do also. A related finding is that when kids do engage in delinquent behavior, they most often do it in the company of their peers. This has led a lot of criminologists to speculate that kids are influencing each other's behavior in negative ways, either through "peer pressure" or some other kind of influence.

I'm mostly interested in another type of peer influence, which is peer influence in a "positive" direction. We know this happens, and we see it when friends don't let friends drive drunk, when someone breaks up a fight, or when a friend talks someone out of doing something that could get them into trouble. How many times does Hermione Granger stop Harry Potter from zapping Draco Malfoy with a spell? That's the kind of thing (in real life, of course) I'm interested in studying. Interestingly, no criminologists have yet studied positive peer influence in a systematic way.

I am also interested in learning more about how, exactly, peers might have a negative influence on each other's behavior, because this is also something that hasn't been studied much in the field of criminology.

In exchange for your help with my research, I'm offering you two percentage points on your final grade for the course for writing a short paper about your experience with peer influence. It's important for you to note that this assignment is **completely voluntary**, and you are not required to complete it. If you'd like to earn some extra credit but you do not want to complete this paper assignment, we can work out **an alternative extra credit assignment** that will involve writing a short paper on a different topic that is related to the course, and that you find interesting. Due to rules protecting "human subjects" of research, you **must be at least 18 years old** to participate in my research project. If you are not 18, and/or if you'd like to do an alternative assignment, just send me an email and we'll choose an alternative topic together. The alternative assignment will also be worth two percentage points on your final grade, and it will also have a due date of Wednesday, October 28.

Paper Guidelines

You have two choices for the paper. Either describe one incident of positive peer influence you were involved in or that you witnessed and one incident of negative peer influence, or describe two incidents of positive peer influence that you were involved in or directly witnessed. I provide more detail below.

Negative Peer Influence

Describe in as much detail as you can a time when you directly witnessed (whether you were involved or not) a person or group influencing another person or group's behavior in a "negative" direction, that is, toward a behavior that is illegal, deviant, risky, or otherwise not a good idea. You can choose an incident in which the influence was successful (the person or group being influenced actually engaged in the negative behavior), or an incident in which the influence was attempted but not successful. But be sure to indicate whether it was successful or not.

Next, discuss the nature of the relationship between the parties involved, if you know. Are these people acquaintances, friends, close friends, romantic partners, siblings, etc.? Is it a close relationship between people who have known each other for a while, or not?

Positive Peer Influence

Describe in as much detail as you can a time when you directly witnessed (whether you were involved or not) a person or group influencing another person or group's behavior in a "positive" direction, that is, trying to get someone to not do something negative as described above, trying to get someone to stop doing something they were doing that was negative, or trying to get someone to do something that was a good thing to do. You can choose an incident in which the influence was successful (the person or group being influenced actually engaged in the negative behavior), or an incident in which the influence was attempted but not successful. Be sure to indicate whether it was successful or not.

Next, discuss the nature of the relationship between the parties involved, if you know. Are these people acquaintances, friends, close friends, romantic partners, siblings, etc.? Is it a close relationship between people who have known each other for a while, or not?

Further Details

Be sure to be very detailed in your accounts, and try to include as much dialogue between the relevant parties as you can—who said what to whom is just as important as who did what.

I'm using the term "peer influence" very loosely. Sometimes there is very little actual peer "influence" toward certain behaviors, such as when one person makes a suggestion that the other person readily agrees to.

I do not consider interaction between "offenders" and "victims" to be examples of peer influence. For example, if someone challenges you to a fight and you fight him or her, the challenge to fight is not what I'm considering peer influence. Rather, if you had friends that either tried to stop the fight or encouraged you to fight, that would be the kind of influence of interest here.

Keep in Mind

Maintain your anonymity and that of people you are writing about—use pseudonyms for you and your friends so no one can tell who you're writing about. As discussed below, **your name should not be on your paper**.

The incidents you describe need not be dramatic or exciting—I'm interested in the full range of peer influence, even "mundane" events. Also, don't write about incidents that you find upsetting to recall—I'm hoping you'll have a little fun writing these papers, and I don't want you to write about things that are difficult for you to write about.

Formatting and Submitting Your Papers

1. Your papers must not have your name on them! Instead, at the time you submit your paper, you will also submit a signed consent form that indicates that you have agreed to allow me to use your papers in my research. This way, you can get credit for completing a paper, but I won't be able to identify you by your papers.
2. Papers should be typed, double-spaced, with reasonable margins, and should be around two-pages in length—you want to be sure to include as much detail as you can about the incidents you're describing. Papers must be **stapled**.
3. Late papers or emailed papers will not be accepted—an emailed paper cannot be anonymous, and I also need to have a signed consent form from you.

Of course, feel free to contact me with any questions you have about the assignment or my research.

APPENDIX B

Questionnaire Administered to URI and OU 2012 Samples

Part I. Background Information

1. What is your sex?

   _____ male

   _____ female

2. How old are you?

   _____ 18

   _____ 19

   _____ 20

   _____ 21

   _____ 22

   _____ 23 or older

3. What is your year in school?

   _____ freshman

   _____ sophomore

   _____ junior

   _____ senior

   _____ other (non-matriculating, for example)

4. What is your race/ethnicity (check all that apply)?

_____ Asian

_____ Black/African-American

_____ Hispanic

_____ Native American/American Indian

_____ White

_____ Other

5. What is your college GPA? _____

6. Which of the following best describes your parents' educational level?

_____ both of my parents have a college (BA, BS) degree or higher

_____ one of my parents has a college (BA, BS) degree or higher

_____ neither of my parents have a college (BA, BS) degree

7. Are you in a fraternity or sorority, or currently pledging to join?

_____ yes

_____ no

8. Where are you currently living?

_____ on campus in a dorm or apartment

_____ on campus in a fraternity or sorority house

_____ off campus, with roommates or by yourself

_____ off campus, with a spouse, girlfriend, boyfriend, and/or children

_____ off campus, with parents or other relative(s)

Part II. Friends   For this Part of the Survey, Think about the People You Consider Your Best Friends, Not Just People Who Are Acquaintances

9. Which of the following best describes the sex composition of your group of best friends?

_____ they are all female

_____ they are mostly female, with some males

_____ they are an equal balance of females and males

_____ they are mostly male, with some females

_____ they are all male

10. In the past year, how many times have you tried to . . .
    Response Categories: "Never, once or twice, several times, many times."

    . . . prevent a friend from driving after drinking alcohol or using drugs?
    . . . get a friend to stop drinking or using drugs after he or she was already intoxicated?
    . . . keep a friend from going home with a person that he or she had just met?
    . . . keep a friend from cheating on his or her boyfriend, girlfriend, or spouse?
    . . . prevent or break up a physical fight that one or more of your friends was involved in?
    . . . prevent or stop a friend from doing an illegal activity not mentioned previously?
    . . . get a friend to drive more slowly or more carefully?
    . . . discourage a friend from skipping a class or "blowing off" schoolwork?

11. When you've tried to prevent or stop a friend/friends from doing the things mentioned above, how often have you been successful?

    _____ always or almost always

    _____ most of the time

    _____ about half of the time

    _____ not that often

    _____ never or almost never

    _____ I have not tried to prevent a friend from doing any of the things mentioned above.

12. In the past year, how many times have you . . .

    . . . encouraged a friend to work harder at school?
    . . . encouraged a friend to wear a seatbelt or bicycle helmet?
    . . . encouraged a friend to eat better?
    . . . encouraged a friend to exercise more?
    . . . encouraged a friend to stop or cut down on an unhealthy habit, like smoking, drinking, or drug use?

13. When you've tried to encourage a friend to do the things mentioned above, how often have you been successful?

    _____ always or almost always

    _____ a good amount of the time

    _____ about half of the time

    _____ not that often

    _____ never or almost never

    _____ I have not encouraged a friend to do any of the things mentioned above.

14. In the past year, how many times has a friend tried to . . .

> . . . prevent you from driving after drinking alcohol or using drugs?
> . . . get you to stop drinking or using drugs after you were already intoxicated?
> . . . keep you from going home with a person that you had just met?
> . . . keep you from cheating on your boyfriend, girlfriend, or spouse?
> . . . prevent or break up a physical fight that you were involved in?
> . . . prevent or stop you from doing an illegal activity not mentioned previously?
> . . . get you to drive more slowly or more carefully?
> . . . discourage you from skipping a class or "blowing off" schoolwork?

15. When a friend has tried to prevent you from doing the things mentioned above, how often has he or she been successful?

_____ always or almost always

_____ most of the time

_____ about half of the time

_____ not that often

_____ never or almost never

_____ I have not had a friend try to prevent me from doing any of the things mentioned above.

16. In the past year, how many times has a friend . . .

> . . . encouraged you to work harder at school?
> . . . encouraged you to wear a seatbelt or bicycle helmet?
> . . . encouraged you to eat better?
> . . . encouraged you to exercise more?
> . . . encouraged you to stop or cut down on an unhealthy habit, like smoking, drinking, or drug use?

17. When a friend has encouraged you do the things mentioned above, how often has he or she been successful?

_____ always or almost always

_____ a good amount of the time

_____ about half of the time

_____ not that often

_____ never or almost never

_____ I have not had a friend encourage me to do any of the things mentioned above.

18. I respect my friends' opinions about the important things in life.

_____ Strongly agree

_____ Agree

_____ Undecided

_____ Disagree

_____ Strongly disagree

19. I know I can count on my friends to help me if I need them.

_____ Strongly agree

_____ Agree

_____ Undecided

_____ Disagree

_____ Strongly disagree

20. I care about my friends' opinions of me.

_____ Strongly agree

_____ Agree

_____ Undecided

_____ Disagree

_____ Strongly disagree

21. How many of your best friends smoke cigarettes daily?

_____ None

_____ One

_____ Two

_____ Three or more

_____ I don't know

22. How many of your best friends have had five or more drinks in a row (in a four hour period) within the past week?

_____ None

_____ One

_____ Two

_____ Three or more

_____ I don't know

23. How many of your friends have used marijuana or hashish in the past week?

_____ None

_____ One

_____ Two

_____ Three or more

_____ I don't know

24. Considering friends who are currently students, how many of them have skipped a class in the past week?

_____ None

_____ One

_____ Two

_____ Three or more

_____ I don't know

_____ I don't have any friends who are students

25. How many of your friends have ever been picked up by the police or arrested?

_____ None

_____ One

_____ Two

_____ Three or more

_____ I don't know

Part III. Your Behavior

Response Categories: "Never, once or twice, several times, many times."

26. How many times in the past year have you . . .

    . . . cheated on a test or homework assignment?
    . . . taken little things (worth less than $5) that didn't belong to you?
    . . . taken things of some value (worth more than $5) that didn't belong to you?
    . . . driven a vehicle after you had been drinking?

. . . been in a physical fight?

. . . gone home with a person you had just met?

. . . cheated on your boyfriend/girlfriend/spouse?

. . . gotten a traffic ticket for a moving violation like speeding?

. . . had a car, truck, or motorcycle accident while you were driving?

. . . been hurt riding your bicycle, skateboarding, rollerblading, snowboarding, etc.?

. . . been to the emergency room of a hospital because of injuries due to an accident?

27. How many times in the past 30 days have you . . .

. . . used marijuana or hashish?

. . . used prescription drugs that were not prescribed for you, like Ritalin, Adderall, pain killers, etc.?

. . . used other drugs (like cocaine, ecstasy, heroin, LSD, steroids, etc.)?

. . . had five or more drinks in a row (within a four-hour period)?

. . . smoked cigarettes?

. . . driven or ridden in a car without a seatbelt on?

Part IV. Your Beliefs and Attitudes

Response Categories: "strongly agree, agree, undecided, disagree, and strongly disagree."

28. Whatever I do, I try hard.
29. I am usually pretty cautious.
30. I don't devote much thought and effort to preparing for the future.
31. An easy life is a happy life.
32. I lose my temper easily.
33. I see no need for hard work.
34. I live for today and let tomorrow take care of itself.
35. Sometimes I take a risk just for the fun of it.
36. It's okay to get around the law if you can get away with it.
37. Most things people call criminal don't really hurt anyone.
38. To get ahead, you have to do some things that are not right.
39. Rules were made to be broken.
40. Only fools tell the truth all the time.

Part V. Parents and School

Response Categories: "strongly agree, agree, undecided, disagree, and strongly disagree."

41. I talk over my future plans with my parents.
42. I would like to be the kind of person my mother is.
43. I would like to be the kind of person my father is.
44. My parents seem to understand me.
45. My parents would stick by me if I got into really bad trouble.

46. I have sometimes felt unwanted by my parents.
47. In general, I like school.
48. I care what my professors think of me.
49. It is important to me to get good grades.
50. I try hard in school.
51. I usually finish my schoolwork on time.
52. On average, not including time spent in classes, how many hours per week do you spend studying or doing other schoolwork?

    _____ 5 hours or less

    _____ 6–10 hours

    _____ 11–15 hours

    _____ 16–20 hours

    _____ Over 20 hours

53. Please describe a recent incident you directly witnessed or participated in that involved "positive" peer influence—where one person/group tried to prevent or stop another person/group from engaging in behavior that could have been problematic. Please do not use anyone's real name in your description, instead, make up names to refer to yourself and/or others.
54. Please describe a recent incident you directly witnessed or participated in that involved "negative" peer influence—where one person/group tried to encourage another person/group to engage in a behavior that could have been problematic. Again, please do not use anyone's real name in your description.

    Thank you very much for your participation!

55. Do you have any additional comments about any of the things we asked you about in the survey?

APPENDIX C

Composition of Indexes Used in Quantitative Analysis

Attempts at Peer Informal Social Control

Response categories:

1 = "never"
2 = "once or twice"
3 = "several times"
4 = "many times"

Receiving Control
(range 12–46, mean 18.16, SD 4.73, Alpha = 0.78)

Has a friend ever tried to prevent you from driving after you had been drinking alcohol or using drugs?

Has a friend ever tried to get you to stop drinking or using drugs after you were already intoxicated?

Has a friend ever tried to keep you from going home with a person that you had just met?

Have you ever tried to keep a friend from cheating on his/her boyfriend, girlfriend, or spouse?*

Has a friend ever tried to prevent or break up a physical fight that you were involved in?

Has a friend ever tried to prevent or stop you from doing an illegal activity not mentioned previously?

Has a friend ever tried to get you to drive more slowly or more carefully?

Has a friend ever tried to discourage you from skipping class or "blowing off" school work?

Has a friend ever encouraged you to work harder at school?

Has a friend ever encouraged you to wear a seatbelt or bicycle/motorcycle helmet?

Has a friend ever encouraged you to eat better?

Has a friend ever encouraged you to exercise more?

Has a friend ever encouraged you to stop or cut down on an unhealthy habit, like smoking, drinking, or drug use?

Administering Control
(range 13–49, mean 25.52, SD 6.70, Alpha = 0.83)

Have you ever tried to prevent a friend from driving after he/she had been drinking alcohol or using drugs?

Have you ever tried to get a friend to stop drinking or using drugs after he or she was already intoxicated?

Have you ever tried to keep a friend from going home with a person that he or she had just met?

Have you ever tried to keep a friend from cheating on his/her boyfriend, girlfriend, or spouse?

Have you ever tried to break up a physical fight that one or more of your friends was involved in?

Have you ever tried to prevent or stop a friend from doing an illegal activity not mentioned previously?

Have you ever tried to get a friend to drive more slowly or more carefully?

Have you ever tried to discourage a friend from skipping class or "blowing off" schoolwork?

Have you ever encouraged a friend to work harder at school?

Have you ever encouraged a friend to wear a seatbelt or bicycle/motorcycle helmet?

Have you ever encouraged a friend to eat better?

Have you ever encouraged a friend to exercise more?

Have you ever encouraged a friend to stop or cut down on an unhealthy habit, like smoking, drinking, or drug use?

* Item had loading score of less than 0.45, so was not included in the scale.

"Success" of Attempts at Peer Informal Social Control

Response categories:

    1 = "never or almost never"
    2 = "not that often"
    3 = "about half the time"
    4 = "most of the time"
    5 = "always or almost always"

Receiving Control Success
(range 2–10, mean 7.25, SD 1.75)

When a friend has tried to prevent or stop you from doing the things mentioned above, how often has he or she been successful?

When a friend has encouraged you to do the things mentioned above, how often has he or she been successful?

Administering Control Success
(range 2–10, mean 6.65, SD 1.60)

When you've tried to prevent or stop a friend from doing the things mentioned above, how often have you been successful?
When you've tried to encourage a friend to do the things mentioned above, how often have you been successful?

Social Control

Peer Attachment
(range 5–15, mean 13.06, SD 1.67, Alpha = 0.70)

Five-point scale, strongly agree through strongly disagree, with high scores indicating stronger peer attachment

I respect my friends' opinions about the important things in life.
I know I can count on my friends to help me if I need them.
I care about my friends' opinions of me.

Parental Attachment
(range 6–30, mean 23.15, SD 5.02, Alpha = 0.81)

Five-point scale, strongly agree through strongly disagree, with high scores indicating stronger parental attachment

I talk over my future plans with my parents.
I would like to be the kind of person my mother is.
I would like to be the kind of person my father is.
My parents seem to understand me.
My parents would stick by me if I got into really bad trouble.
I have sometimes felt unwanted by my parents. (reverse coded)

School Attachment (Standardized)
(range −18.39–7.51, mean .03, SD 4.67, Alpha = 0.79)

Items recoded as need so that high scores indicate stronger school attachment

In general, do you like or dislike school? (like, like and dislike equally, dislike)
Do you care what your professors think of you? (I care a lot, I care some, I don't care)
How important is getting good grades to you? (very, somewhat, a little, not at all)
I try hard in school. (five-point scale, strongly agree through strongly disagree)
I usually finish my schoolwork. (five-point scale, strongly agree through strongly disagree)
What is your college GPA?

Belief
(range 5–25, mean 19.03, SD 4.06, Alpha = 0.81)

Five-point scale, strongly agree through strongly disagree, with high scores indicating stronger peer attachment

It's okay to get around the law if you can get away with it.
Most things people call criminal don't really hurt anyone.
To get ahead, you have to do some things that are not right.
Rules were made to be broken.
Only fools tell the truth all the time.

Self-Control

Attitudinal Measure
(range 7–25, mean 19.92, SD 2.86, Alpha = 0.56)

Five-point scale, strongly agree through strongly disagree, high scores indicating higher self-control

Whatever I do, I try hard.
I don't devote much thought and effort to preparing for the future.
An easy life is a happy life.
I see no need for hard work.
I live for today and let tomorrow take care of itself.

Behavioral Measure
(range 7–16, mean 15.33, SD 1.07, Alpha = 0.48)

Response categories:

   1 = "many times"
   2 = "several times"
   3 = "once or twice"
   4 = "never"

How many times in the past year have you. . .

Gotten a traffic ticket for a moving violation like speeding?
Had a car, truck, or motorcycle accident while you were driving?
Been hurt riding your bicycle, or while skateboarding, rollerblading, snowboarding, etc.?
Been to the emergency room of a hospital because of injuries due to an accident?

Friends' Deviance

Response categories:

> 0 = "none"
> 1 = "one"
> 2 = "two"
> 3 = "three or more"

Peer Deviance
(range 0–12, mean 4.04, SD 3.65, Alpha = 0.73)

How many of your friends smoke cigarettes daily?
Within the past week, how many of your best friends have had five or more drinks in a row (in a four-hour period)?
How many of your friends have used marijuana or hashish in the past week?
Considering your friends who are also students, how many of them have skipped a class in the past week?*
How many of your friends have ever been picked up by the police or arrested?

Respondent Deviance

Response categories:

> 0 = "never"
> 1 = "once or twice"
> 2 = "several times"
> 3 = "many times"

Respondent Deviance
(range 0–24, mean 2.86, SD 3.83, Alpha = 0.78)

How many times in the past year have you taken little things (worth less than $5) that didn't belong to you?
How many times in the past year have you taken things of some value (worth more than $5) that didn't belong to you?
How many times in the past year have you driven a vehicle after you had been drinking?
How many times in the past year have you been in a physical fight?
How many times in the past year have you gone home with a person you had just met?
How many times in the past 30 days have you used marijuana or hashish?
How many times in the past 30 days have you used prescription drugs recreationally (Ritalin, Adderall, pain killers, etc.)?

How many times in the past 30 days have you used other drugs (like cocaine, ecstasy, heroin, LSD, steroids, etc.)?

How many times in the past 30 days have you had more than five drinks in a row (within a four-hour period)?

How many times in the past 30 days have you smoked cigarettes?

★ Item had loading score of less than 0.45, so was not included in the scale.

REFERENCES

Agnew, Robert. 1993. "Why Do They Do It? An Examination of the Intervening Mechanisms Between "Social Control" Variables and Delinquency." *Journal of Research in Crime and Delinquency* 30(3):245–66.

Akers, Ronald L. 1996. "Is Differential Association/Social Learning Cultural Deviance Theory?" *Criminology* 34(2):229–47.

Akers, Ronald L. 1998. *Social Learning and Social Structure: A General Theory of Crime and Deviance.* New Brunswick, NJ: Transaction Publishers.

Alarid, Leanne Fiftal, Vlemer S. Burton, and Francis T. Cullen. 2000. "Gender and Crime among Felony Offenders: Assessing the Generality of Social Control and Differential Association Theories." *Journal of Research in Crime and Delinquency* 37(2):171–99.

Allen, Joseph P. and Jill Antonishak. 2008. "Adolescent Peer Influences: Beyond the Dark Side." Pp. 141–60 in *Understanding Peer Influence in Children and Adolescents*, edited by M. J. Prinstein and K. A. Dodge. New York, NY: Guilford.

Altermatt, Ellen Rydell. 2012. "Children's Achievement-Related Discourse with Peers: Uncovering the Processes of Peer Influence." Pp. 109–34 in *Peer Relationships and Adjustment at School*, edited by A. M. Ryan and G. W. Ladd. Charlotte, NC: Information Age Publishing.

Anderson, Elijah. 1999. *Code of the Street: Decency, Violence, and the Moral Life of the Inner City.* New York, NY: W.W. Norton and Company, Inc.

Andrews, Judy A., Elizabeth Tildesley, Hyman Hops, and Fuzhong Li. 2002. "The Influence of Peers on Young Adult Substance Use." *Health Psychology* 21(4):349–57.

Armstrong, Elizabeth A., Laura Hamilton, and Brian Sweeney. 2006. "Sexual Assault on Campus: A Multilevel, Integrative Approach to Party Rape." *Social Problems* 53(4):483–99.

Asch, Solomon E. 1956. "Studies of Independence and Conformity: 1. A Minority of One Against a Unanimous Majority." *Psychological Monographs: General and Applied* 70:1–70.

Baer, John S., Alan Stacy, and Mary Larimer. 1991. "Biases in the Perception of Drinking Norms among College Students." *Journal of Studies on Alcohol and Drugs* 52(6):580–86.

Banyard, Victoria L., Elizabethe G. Plante, and Mary M. Moynihan. 2004. "Bystander Education: Bringing a Broader Community Perspective to Sexual Violence Prevention." *Journal of Community Psychology* 32(1):61–79.

Banyard, Victoria L., Mary M. Moynihan, and Elizabethe G. Plante. 2007. "Sexual Violence Prevention through Bystander Education: An Experimental Evaluation." *Journal of Community Psychology* 35(4):463–81.

Barry, Carolyn McNamara and Kathryn R. Wentzel. 2006. "Friend Influence on Prosocial Behavior: The Role of Motivational Factors and Friendship Characteristics." *Developmental Psychology* 42(1):153–63.

Berndt, Thomas J. and Keunho Keefe. 1995. "Friends' Influence on Adolescents' Adjustment to School." *Child Development* 66(5):1312–29.

Berndt, Thomas J. and Lonna M. Murphy. 2002. "Influences of Friends and Friendships: Myths, Truths, and Research Recommendations." Pp. 275–310 in *Advances in Child Development and Behavior, Vol. 30*, edited by R. V. Kail. Boston, MA: Academic.

Black, Donald. 1993. *The Social Structure of Right and Wrong*. San Diego, CA: Academic Press.

Boman, John H., IV, John M. Stogner, Bryan Lee Miller, O. Hayden Griffin III, and Marvin D. Krohn. 2012. "On the Operational Validity of Perceptual Peer Delinquency: Exploring Projection and Elements Contained in Perceptions." *Journal of Research in Crime and Delinquency* 49(4):601–21.

Bourgeois, Martin J. and Anne Bowen. 2001. "Self-Organization of Alcohol-Related Attitudes and Beliefs in a Campus Housing Complex: An Initial Investigation." *Health Psychology* 20(6):434–37.

Brechwald, Whitney A. and Mitchell J. Prinstein. 2011. "Beyond Homophily: A Decade of Advances in Understanding Peer Influence Processes." *Journal of Research on Adolescence* 21(1):166–79.

Briar, Scott and Irving Piliavin. 1965. "Delinquency, Situational Inducements, and Commitment to Conformity." *Social Problems* 13(1):35–45.

Brown, B. Bradford and Christa Klute. 2003. "Friendships, Cliques, and Crowds." Pp. 330–48 in *Blackwell Handbook of Adolescence*, edited by G. R. Adams and M. D. Berzonsky. Malden, MA: Blackwell Publishing.

Brown, B. Bradford, Donna Rae Clasen, and Sue Ann Eicher. 1986. "Perceptions of Peer Pressure, Peer Conformity Dispositions, and Self-Reported Behavior Among Adolescents." *Developmental Psychology* 22(4):521–30.

Brown, B. Bradford, Jeremy P. Bakken, Suzanne W. Ameringer, and Shelly D. Mahon. 2008. "A Comprehensive Conceptualization of the Peer Influence Process in Adolescence." Pp. 17–44 in *Understanding Peer Influence in Children and Adolescents*, edited by M. J. Prinstein and K. A. Dodge. New York, NY: Guilford.

Bruinsma, Gerben. 1992. "Differential Association Theory Reconsidered: An Extension and Its Empirical Test." *Journal of Quantitative Criminology* 8(1):29–49.

Bukowski, William M., Andrew F. Newcomb, and Willard W. Hartup. 1996. "Friendship and Its Significance in Childhood and Adolescence: Introduction and Comment." Pp. 1–15 in *The Company They Keep: Friendships in Childhood and Adolescence*, edited by W. M. Bukowski, A. F. Newcomb, and W. W. Hartup. New York, NY: Cambridge University Press.

Burgess, Robert L. and Ronald L. Akers. 1966. "A Differential Association-Reinforcement Theory of Criminal Behavior." *Social Problems* 14(2):128–47.

Burkett, Steven R. and Eric L. Jensen. 1975. "Conventional Ties, Peer Influence, and the Fear of Apprehension: A Study of Adolescent Marijuana Use." *The Sociological Quarterly* 16(4):522–33.

Burt, Cyril. 1925. *The Young Delinquent*. New York, NY: D. Appleton and Company.

Cairns, Robert B. and Beverly D. Cairns. 1994. *Lifelines and Risks: Pathways of Youth in Our Time*. New York, NY: Cambridge University Press.

Callimachi, Rukmini. 2015. "ISIS and the Lonely Young American." *The New York Times*, June 27. Retrieved July 19, 2015 (http://nyti.ms/1NnFoZb).

Chamlin, Mitchell B. and John K. Cochran. 1997. "Social Altruism and Crime." *Criminology* 35(2):203–26.

Chapple, Constance. 2005. "Self-Control, Peer Relations, and Delinquency." *Justice Quarterly* 22(1):89–106.

Cillessen, Antonius H. N. and Lara Mayeux. 2004. "Sociometric Status and Peer Group Behavior: Previous Findings and Current Directions." Pp. 3–20 in *Children's Peer Relations: From Development to Intervention*, edited by J. B. Kupersmidt and K. A. Dodge. Washington, DC: American Psychological Association.

Cissner, Amanda B. 2009. "Evaluating the Mentors in Violence Prevention Program." *Center for Court Innovation*. Retrieved June 15, 2015 (http://justideasonline.org/sites/default/files/MVP_evaluation.pdf).

Clasen, Donna Rae and B. Bradford Brown. 1985. "The Multidimensionality of Peer Pressure in Adolescence." *Journal of Youth and Adolescence* 14(6):451–68.

Cloward, Richard and Lloyd Ohlin. 1960. *Delinquency and Opportunity: A Theory of Delinquent Gangs*. Glencoe, IL: Free Press.

Cohen, Albert K. 1955. *Delinquent Boys: The Culture of the Gang*. New York, NY: Free Press.

Cohen, Lawrence E. and Marcus Felson. 1979. "Social Change and Crime Rate Trends: A Routine Activity Approach." *American Sociological Review* 44(4):588–608.

Coie, John D. and Janis B. Kupersmidt. 1983. "A Behavioral Analysis of Emerging Social Status in Boys' Groups." *Child Development* 54(6):1400–16.

Colvin, Mark, Francis T. Cullen, and Thomas Vander Ven. 2002. "Coercion, Social Support, and Crime: An Emerging Theoretical Consensus." *Criminology* 40(1):19–42.

Cooney, Mark. 1998. *Warriors and Peacemakers: How Third Parties Shape Violence*. New York and London: New York University Press.

Costello, Barbara J. 1997. "On the Logical Adequacy of Cultural Deviance Theories." *Theoretical Criminology* 1(4):403–28.

Costello, Barbara J. 2006a. "Cultural Relativism and the Study of Deviance." *Sociological Spectrum* 26(6): 581–94.

Costello, Barbara J. 2006b. "Believe What I Say, Not What I Do: A Rejoinder to Goode." *Sociological Spectrum* 26(6):615–19.

Costello, Barbara. 2010. "Peer Influence Toward Conformity." *Journal of Crime and Justice* 33(1):97–116.

Costello, Barbara J. and Paul R. Vowell. 1999. "Testing Control Theory and Differential Association: A Reanalysis of the Richmond Youth Project Data." *Criminology* 37(4):815–42.

Cullen, F. T. 1994. "Social support as an organizing concept for criminology. Presidential address to the Academy of Criminal Justice Sciences." *Justice Quarterly*, 11:527–59.

Decker, Scott H. and Barrik Van Winkle. 1996. *Life in the Gang: Family, Friends, and Violence*. Cambridge, UK: Cambridge University Press.

DeLisi, Matt. 2001. "It's All in the Record: Assessing Self-Control Theory with an Offender Sample. *Criminal Justice Review* 26(1):1–16.

Dishion, Thomas J. and Gerald R. Patterson. 2006. "The Development and Ecology of Antisocial Behavior in Children and Adolescents." Pp. 503–41 in *Developmental Psychopathology, Second Edition, Volume 3: Risk, Disorder, and Adaptation*, edited by D. Cicchetti and D. J. Cohen. Hoboken, NJ: Wiley and Sons.

Dishion, Thomas J., Kathleen M. Spracklen, David W. Andrews, and Gerald R. Patterson. 1996. "Deviancy Training in Male Adolescent Friendships." *Behavior Therapy* 27(3):373–90.

Dishion, Thomas J., Timothy F. Piehler, and Michael W. Myers. 2008. "Dynamics and Ecology of Adolescent Peer Influence." Pp. 72–93 in *Understanding Peer Influence in Children and Adolescents*, edited by M. J. Prinstein and K. A. Dodge. New York, NY: Guilford Press.

Dodge, Kenneth A. 1983. "Behavioral Antecedents of Peer Social Status." *Child Development* 54(6):1386–89.

Elliott, Delbert S., David Huizinga, and Scott Menard. 1989. *Multiple Problem Youth: Delinquency, Drugs, and Mental Health Problems*. New York, NY: Springer-Verlag.

Elliott, Delbert S., David Huizinga, and Suzanne S. Ageton. 1985. *Explaining Delinquency and Drug Use*. Beverly Hills, LA: Sage.

Ennett, Susan T. and Karl E. Bauman. 1994. "The Contribution of Influence and Selection to Adolescent Peer Group Homogeneity: The Case of Adolescent Cigarette Smoking." *Journal of Personality and Social Psychology* 67(4):653–63.

Ennett, Susan T., Karl E. Bauman, Andrea Hussong, Robert Faris, Vangie A. Foshee, Li Cai and Robert H. DuRant. 2006. "The Peer Context of Adolescent Substance Use: Findings from Social Network Analysis." *Journal of Research on Adolescence* 16(2):159–86.

Epstein, Joyce Levy. 1983. "The Influence of Friends on Achievement and Affective Outcomes." Pp. 177–200 in *Friends in School: Patterns of Selection and Influence in Secondary Schools*, edited by J. L. Epstein and N. Karweit. New York, NY: Academic Press.

Erickson, Maynard L. 1971. "The Group Context of Delinquent Behavior." *Social Problems* 19(1):114–29.

Felson, Marcus. 2003. "The Process of Co-offending." *Crime Prevention Studies* 16:149–68.

Felson, Richard B. 1982. "Impression Management and the Escalation of Aggression and Violence." *Social Psychology Quarterly* 45(4):245–54.

Felson, Richard B. and Henry J. Steadman. 1983. "Situational Factors in Disputes Leading to Criminal Violence." *Criminology* 21(1):59–74.

Felson, Richard B., Allen E. Liska, Scott J. South, and Thomas L. McNulty. 1994. "The Subculture of Violence and Delinquency: Individual vs. School Context Effects." *Social Forces* 73(1):155–73.

Fisher, Bonnie S., John J. Sloan, Francis T. Cullen, and Chunmeng Lu. 1998. "Crime in the Ivory Tower: The Level and Sources of Student Victimization." *Criminology* 36(3):671–710.

Flanagan, Constance A., Elvira Elek-Fisk, and Leslie S. Gallay. 2004. "Friends Don't Let Friends . . . Or Do They? Developmental and Gender Differences in Intervening in Friends' ATOD Use." *Journal of Drug Education* 34(4):351–71.

Fleisher, Mark S. 2006. "Youth Gang Social Dynamics and Social Network Analysis: Applying Degree Centrality Measures to Assess the Nature of Gang Boundaries." Pp. 85–99 in *Studying Youth Gangs*, edited by J. F. Short, Jr. and L. A. Hughes. Lanham, MD: AltaMira.

Freeman, Linton C. 2004. *The Development of Social Network Analysis: A Study in the Sociology of Science. Vol. 1.* Vancouver, Canada: Empirical Press.

Furman, Wyndol and Valerie A. Simon. 2008. "Homophily in Adolescent Romantic Relationships." Pp. 203–24 in *Understanding Peer Influence in Children and Adolescents*, edited by M. J. Prinstein and K. A. Dodge. New York, NY: Guilford Press.

Gardner, LeGrande and Donald J. Shoemaker. 1989. "Social Bonding and Delinquency: A Comparative Analysis." *The Sociological Quarterly* 30(3):481–99.

Gifford-Smith, Mary, Kenneth A. Dodge, Thomas J. Dishion, and Joan McCord. 2005. "Peer Influence in Children and Adolescents: Crossing the Bridge from Developmental to Intervention Science." *Journal of Abnormal Child Psychology* 33(3):255–65.

Giordano, Peggy C., Robert A. Lonardo, Wendy D. Manning, and Monica A. Longmore. 2010. "Adolescent Romance and Delinquency: A Further Exploration of Hirschi's "Cold and Brittle" Relationships Hypothesis." *Criminology* 48(4):919–46.

Giordano, Peggy C., Stephen A. Cernkovich, and Meredith D. Pugh. 1986. "Friendships and Delinquency." *American Journal of Sociology* 91(5):1170–202.

Glueck, Sheldon and Eleanor Glueck. 1950. *Unraveling Juvenile Delinquency*. Cambridge, MA: Harvard University Press.

Goff, Brent G. and H. Wallace Goddard. 1999. "Terminal Core Values Associated with Adolescent Problem Behaviors." *Adolescence* 34(133):47–60.

Gottfredson, Michael R. and Travis Hirschi. 1990. *A General Theory of Crime*. Stanford, CA: Stanford University Press.

Hamm, Jill V., Abigail Hoffman, and Thomas W. Farmer. 2012. "Peer Cultures of Academic Effort and Achievement in Adolescence: Why They Matter, and What Teachers Can Do About Them." Pp. 219–50 in *Peer Relationships and Adjustment at School*, edited by A. M. Ryan and G. W. Ladd. Charlotte, NC: Information Age Publishing.

Hartup, Willard W. 1992. "Friendships and Their Developmental Significance." Pp. 175–202 in *Childhood Social Development: Contemporary Perspectives*, edited by H. McGurk. East Sussex, UK: Lawrence Erlbaum Associates.

Haynie, Dana L. 2001. "Delinquent Peers Revisited: Does Network Structure Matter?" *American Journal of Sociology* 106(4):1013–57.

Haynie, Dana L. and D. Wayne Osgood. 2005. "Reconsidering Peers and Delinquency: How Do Peers Matter?" *Social Forces* 84(2):1109–30.

Haynie, Dana L., Peggy C. Giordano, Wendy D. Manning and Monica A. Longmore. 2005. "Adolescent Romantic Relationships and Delinquency Involvement." *Criminology* 43(1):177–210.

Heimer, Karen. 1996. "Gender, Interaction, and Delinquency: Testing a Theory of Differential Social Control." *Social Psychology Quarterly* 59(1):39–61.

Hernandez, Anthony C. R., Michael D. Newcomb, and Jerome Rabow. 1995. "Types of Drunk-Driving Intervention: Prevalence, Success and Gender." *Journal of Studies on Alcohol* 56(4):408–413.

Hindelang, Michael J. 1973. "Causes of Delinquency: A Partial Replication and Extension." *Social Problems* 20(4):471–87.

Hirschi, Travis. 1969 [2002]. *Causes of Delinquency*. Berkeley, CA: University of California Press.

Hirschi, Travis. 1996. "Theory Without Ideas: Reply to Akers." *Criminology* 34(2):249–56.

Hirschi, Travis. 2004. "Self-Control and Crime." Pp. 537–52 in *Handbook of Self-Regulation: Research, Theory, and Applications*, edited by R. F. Baumeister and K. D. Vohs. New York, NY: The Guilford Press.

Jaccard, James, Hart Blanton, and Tonya Dodge. 2005. "Peer Influences on Risk Behavior: An Analysis of the Effects of a Close Friend." *Developmental Psychology* 41(1):135–47.

Jensen, Gary F. 1972. "Parents, Peers, and Delinquent Action: A Test of the Differential Association Perspective." *American Journal of Sociology* 78(3):562–75.

Johnson, Richard E., Anastasios C. Marcos, and Stephen J. Bahr. 1987. "The Role of Peers in the Complex Etiology of Adolescent Drug Use." *Criminology* 25(2):323–40.

Johnston, Lloyd D., Patrick M. O'Malley, Jerald G. Bachman, and John E. Schulenberg. 2012. *Monitoring the Future National Results on Adolescent Drug Use: Overview of Key Findings, 2011*. Ann Arbor, MI: Institute for Social Research, University of Michigan.

Jones, Edward E. 1964. *Ingratiation: A Social Psychological Analysis*. New York, NY: Appleton-Century-Crofts.

Jones, Edward E. and Victor A. Harris. 1967. "The Attribution of Attitudes." *Journal of Experimental Social Psychology* 3:1–24.

Jussim, Lee and D. Wayne Osgood. 1989. "Influence and Similarity among Friends: An Integrative Model Applied to Incarcerated Adolescents." *Social Psychology Quarterly* 52(2):98–112.

Kandel, Denise B. 1978. "Homophily, Selection, and Socialization in Adolescent Friendships." *American Journal of Sociology* 84(2):427–36.

Kandel, Denise and Mark Davies. 1991. "Friendship Networks, Intimacy, and Illicit Drug Use in Young Adulthood: A Comparison of Two Competing Theories." *Criminology* 29(3):441–69.

Katz, Jackson. 2015. "Mentors in Violence Prevention (MVP)." Retrieved June 18, 2015 (http://jacksonkatz.com/aboutmvp.html).

Kirk, David S. and Andrew V. Papachristos. 2011. "Cultural Mechanisms and the Persistence of Neighborhood Violence." *American Journal of Sociology* 116(4):1190–233.

Kornhauser, Ruth Rosner. 1978. *Social Sources of Delinquency: An Appraisal of Analytic Models*. Chicago, IL: University of Chicago Press.

Krohn, Marvin D. and James L. Massey. 1980. "Social Control and Delinquent Behavior: An Examination of the Elements of the Social Bond." *The Sociological Quarterly* 21(4):529–44.

LaBrie, Joseph W., Jessica Cail, Justin F. Hummer, Andrew Lac, and Clayton Neighbors. 2009. "What Men Want: The Role of Reflective Opposite-Sex Normative Preferences in Alcohol Use among College Women." *Psychology of Addictive Behaviors* 23(1):157–62.

Langhinrichsen-Rohling, Jennifer, John D. Foubert, Hope M. Brasfield, Brent Hill, and Shannon Shelley-Tremblay. 2011. "The Men's Program: Does It Impact College Men's Self-Reported Bystander Efficacy and Willingness to Intervene?" *Violence Against Women* 17(6):743–59.

Lashbrook, Jeffrey T. 2000. "Fitting in: Exploring the Emotional Dimension of Adolescent Peer Pressure." *Adolescence* 35(140):747–57.

Laub, John H. and Robert J. Sampson. 2003. *Shared Beginnings, Divergent Lives: Delinquent Boys to Age 70*. Cambridge, MA: Harvard University Press.

Lazarsfeld, Paul F. and Robert K. Merton. 1954. "Friendship as a Social Process: A Substantive and Methodological Analysis." *Freedom and Control in Modern Society* 18(1):18–66.

Lombroso-Ferrero, Gina. 1911. *Criminal Man According to the Classification of Cesare Lombroso*. New York, NY: G.P. Putnam's Sons.

Lonardo, Robert A., Peggy C. Giordano, Monica A. Longmore, and Wendy D. Manning. 2009. "Parents, Friends, and Romantic Partners: Enmeshment in Deviant Networks and Adolescent Delinquency Involvement." *Journal of Youth and Adolescence* 38(3):367–83.

Marcus, Bernd. 2003. "An Empirical Examination of the Construct Validity of Two Alternative Self-Control Measures." *Educational and Psychological Measurement* 63(4):674–706.

Martens, Matthew P., Kristen Dams-O'Connor, Christy Duffy-Paiement, and Justin T. Gibson. 2006. "Perceived Alcohol Use among Friends and Alcohol Consumption among College Athletes." *Psychology of Addictive Behaviors* 20(2):178–84.

Matsueda, Ross L. 1982. "Testing Control Theory and Differential Association: A Causal Modeling Approach." *American Sociological Review* 47(4):489–504.

Matsueda, Ross L. and Kathleen Anderson. 1998. "The Dynamics of Delinquent Peers and Delinquent Behavior." *Criminology* 36(2):269–308.

Matza, David. 1964. *Delinquency and Drift.* New York, NY: John Wiley and Sons, Inc.

McGloin, Jean Marie. 2009. "Delinquency Balance: Revisiting Peer Influence." *Criminology* 47(2):439–77.

McGloin, Jean Marie and Holly Nguyen. 2012. "It Was My Idea: Considering the Instigation of Co-offending." *Criminology* 50(2):463–94.

Mercken, Liesbeth, Tom A. B. Snijders, Christian Steglich, Erkki Vartiainen, and Hein De Vries. 2010. "Dynamics of Adolescent Friendship Networks and Smoking Behavior." *Social Networks* 32(1):72–81.

Mermelstein, Robin, Sheldon Cohen, Edward Lichtenstein, John S. Baer, and Tom Kamarck. 1986. "Social Support and Smoking Cessation and Maintenance." *Journal of Consulting and Clinical Psychology* 54(4):447–53.

Miller, Dale T. and Cathy McFarland. 1987. "Pluralistic Ignorance: When Similarity Is Interpreted as Dissimilarity." *Journal of Personality and Social Psychology* 53(2):298–305.

Miller, Walter B. 1958. "Lower Class Culture as a Generating Milieu of Gang Delinquency." *Journal of Social Issues* 14(3):5–19.

Minor, W. William. 1984. "Neutralization as a Hardening Process: Considerations in the Modeling of Change." *Social Forces* 62(4):995–1019.

Neighbors, Clayton, Melissa A. Lewis, Rochelle L. Bergstrom, and Mary E. Larimer. 2006. "Being Controlled by Normative Influences: Self-Determination as a Moderator of a Normative Feedback Alcohol Intervention." *Health Psychology* 25(5):571–79.

Nelson, R. Michael and Teresa K. DeBacker. 2008. "Achievement Motivation in Adolescents: The Role of Peer Climate and Best Friends." *The Journal of Experimental Education* 76(2):170–89.

Oliver, William. 1994. *The Violent Social World of Black Men.* New York, NY: Lexington Books.

Osgood, D. Wayne and Amy L. Anderson. 2004. "Unstructured Socializing and Rates of Delinquency." *Criminology* 42(3):519–50.

Osgood, D. Wayne, Janet K. Wilson, Jerald G. Bachman, Patrick M. O'Malley and Lloyd D. Johnston. 1996. "Routine Activities and Individual Deviant Behavior." *American Sociological Review* 61(4):635–55.

Paternoster, Ray, Jean M. McGloin, Holly Nguyen, and Kyle J. Thomas. 2012. "The Causal Impact of Exposure to Deviant Peers: An Experimental Investigation." *Journal of Research in Crime and Delinquency* 50(4):476–503.

Patterson, Gerald R. and Thomas J. Dishion. 1985. "Contributions of Families and Peers to Delinquency." *Criminology* 23(1):63–79.

Perkins, H. Wesley, Michael P. Haines, and Richard Rice. 2005. "Misperceiving the College Drinking Norm and Related Problems: A Nationwide Study of Exposure to Prevention Information, Perceived Norms and Student Alcohol Misuse." *Journal of Studies on Alcohol and Drugs* 66(4):470–78.

Piquero, Alex R., John MacDonald, Adam Dobrin, Leah E. Daigle, and Francis T. Cullen. 2005. "Self-Control, Violent Offending, and Homicide Victimization: Assessing the General Theory of Crime." *Journal of Quantitative Criminology* 21(1):55–71.

Prentice, Deborah A. 2008. "Mobilizing and Weakening Peer Influence as Mechanisms for Changing Behavior: Implications for Alcohol Intervention Programs." Pp. 161–80 in *Understanding Peer Influence in Children and Adolescents*, edited by M. J. Prinstein and K. A. Dodge. New York, NY: Guilford.

Prinstein, Mitchell J. and Shirley S. Wang. 2005. "False Consensus and Adolescent Peer Contagion: Examining Discrepancies between Perceptions and Actual Reporting Levels of Friends' Deviant and Health Risk Behaviors." *Journal of Abnormal Child Psychology* 33(3):293–306.

Rabow, Jerome, Anthony C. R. Hernandez, and Ronald K. Watts. 1986. "College Students Do Intervene in Drunk Driving Situations." *Sociology and Social Research* 70(3):224–225.

Rabow, Jerome, Michael D. Newcomb, Martin A. Monto, and Anthony C. R. Hernandez. 1990. "Altruism in Drunk Driving Situations: Personal and Situational Factors in Intervention." *Social Psychology Quarterly* 53(3):199–213.

Rebellon, Cesar J. 2006. "Do Adolescents Engage in Delinquency to Attract the Social Attention of Peers? An Extension and Longitudinal Test of the Social Reinforcement Hypothesis." *Journal of Research in Crime and Delinquency* 43(4):387–411.

Rebellon, Cesar J. 2012. "Differential Association and Substance Use: Assessing the Roles of Discriminant Validity, Socialization, and Selection in Traditional Empirical Tests." *European Journal of Criminology* 9(1):73–96.

Rebellon, Cesar J. and Kathryn L. Modecki. 2014. "Accounting for Projection Bias in Models of Delinquent Peer Influence: The Utility and Limits of Latent Variable Approaches." *Journal of Quantitative Criminology* 30(2):163–86.

Reed, Mark D. and Dina R. Rose. 1998. "Doing What Simple Simon Says? Estimating the Underlying Causal Structures of Delinquent Associations, Attitudes, and Serious Theft." *Criminal Justice and Behavior* 25(2):240–74.

Reiss, Albert J. and A. L. Rhodes. 1964. "An Empirical Test of Differential Association Theory." *Journal of Research in Crime and Delinquency* 1(1):5–18.

Resnick, Barbara, Denise Orwig, Jay Magaziner, and Carol Wynne. 2002. "The Effect of Social Support on Exercise Behavior in Older Adults." *Clinical Nursing Research* 11(2):52–70.

Riley, David. 1987. "Time and Crime: The Link Between Teenager Lifestyle and Delinquency." *Journal of Quantitative Criminology* 3(4):339–54.

Roman, Caterina G., Meagan Cahill, Pamela Lachman, Samantha Lowry, Carlena Orosco, Christopher McCarty, Megan Denver, and Juan Pedroza. 2012. "Social Networks, Delinquency, and Gang Membership: Using a Neighborhood Framework to Examine the Influence of Network Composition and Structure in a Latino Community." *The Urban Institute*, Washington, DC. Retrieved May 23, 2014 (www.ncjrs.gov/pdffiles1/ojjdp/grants/238538.pdf).

Rosenbaum, Jill Leslie. 1987. "Social Control, Gender, and Delinquency: An Analysis of Drug, Property, and Violent Offenders." *Justice Quarterly* 4(1):117–32.

Rosenberg, Tina. 2011. *Join the Club: How Peer Pressure Can Transform the World*. New York: W. W. Norton & Company.

Ryan, Allison M. 2000. "Peer Groups as a Context for the Socialization of Adolescents' Motivation, Engagement, and Achievement in School." *Educational Psychologist* 35(2):101–11.

Sageman, Marc. 2004. *Understanding Terror Networks*. Philadelphia, PA: University of Pennsylvania Press.

Salmivalli, Christina, Ari Kaukiainen, and Marinus Voeten. 2005. "Anti-Bullying Intervention: Implementation and Outcome." *British Journal of Educational Psychology* 75(3):465–87.

Sampson, Robert J. and Dawn Jeglum Bartusch. 1998. "Legal Cynicism and (Subcultural?) Tolerance of Deviance: The Neighborhood Context of Racial Differences." *Law and Society Review* 32(4):777–804.

Sampson, Robert J. and John H. Laub. 1993. *Crime in the Making: Pathways and Turning Points Through Life*. Cambridge, MA: Harvard University Press.

Sampson, Robert J. and Lydia Bean. 2006. "Cultural Mechanisms and Killing Fields: A Revised Theory of Community-Level Racial Inequality." Pp. 3–36 in *The Many Colors of Crime: Inequalities of Race, Ethnicity and Crime in America*, edited by R. Peterson, L. Krivo, and J. Hagan. New York, NY: New York University Press.

Sarnecki, Jerzy. 2001. *Delinquent Networks*. Cambridge, MA: Cambridge University Press.

Scheff, Thomas J. 1990. *Microsociology: Discourse, Emotion, and Social Structure*. Chicago, IL: University of Chicago Press.

Shaw, Clifford R. 1931. *The Natural History of a Delinquent Career*. Chicago, IL: University of Chicago Press.

Shaw, Clifford R. and Henry D. McKay. 1942. *Juvenile Delinquency and Urban Areas*. Chicago, IL: University of Chicago Press.

Sherif, Muzafer, Carolyn W. Sherif, and Gardner Murphy. 1964. *Reference Groups: Exploration into Conformity and Deviation of Adolescents.* New York, NY: Harper and Row.

Short, James F. 1957. "Differential Association and Delinquency." *Social Problems* 4(3):233–39.

Simons-Morton, Bruce, Neil Lerner, and Jeremiah Singer. 2005. "The Observed Effects of Teenage Passengers on the Risky Driving Behavior of Teenage Drivers." *Accident Analysis & Prevention* 37(6):973–982.

Soss, Joe, Laura Langbein, and Alan R. Metelko. 2003. "Why Do White Americans Support the Death Penalty?" *The Journal of Politics* 65(2):397–421.

Sutherland, Edwin. 1947. *Principles of Criminology, Fourth Edition.* Philadelphia, PA: Lippincott.

Sutherland, Edwin, Donald R. Cressey, and David F. Luckenbill. 1992. *Principles of Criminology, Eleventh Edition.* Lanham, MD: General Hall.

Swidler, Ann. 1986. "Culture in Action: Symbols and Strategies." *American Sociological Review* 51(2):273–86.

Sykes, Gresham M. and David Matza. 1957. "Techniques of Neutralization: A Theory of Delinquency." *American Sociological Review* 22(6):664–70.

Tabachnick, Barbara G. and Linda S. Fidell. 2007. *Using Multivariate Statistics, Fifth Edition.* Boston, MA: Pearson Education, Inc.

Thornberry, Terence P., Alan J. Lizotte, Marvin D. Krohn, Margaret Farnworth, and Sung Joon Jang. 1994. "Delinquent Peers, Beliefs, and Delinquent Behavior: A Longitudinal Test of Interactional Theory." *Criminology* 32(1):47–83.

Turrisi, Rob, Nadine R. Mastroleo, Kimberly A. Mallett, Mary E. Larimer, and Jason R. Kilmer. 2007. "Examination of the Mediational Influences of Peer Norms, Environmental Influences, and Parent Communications on Heavy Drinking in Athletes and Nonathletes." *Psychology of Addictive Behaviors* 21(4):453–61.

Vasquez, Bob Edward and Gregory M. Zimmerman. 2014. "An Investigation into the Empirical Relationship Between Time Spent with Peers, Friendship, and Delinquency." *Journal of Criminal Justice* 42(3):244–56.

Ward, Jeffrey T., Chris L. Gibson, John Boman, and Walter L. Leite. 2010. "Assessing the Validity of the Retrospective Behavioral Self-Control Scale: Is the General Theory of Crime Stronger Than the Evidence Suggests?" *Criminal Justice and Behavior* 37(3):336–57.

Warr, Mark. 1993. "Parents, Peers, and Delinquency." *Social Forces* 72(1):247–64.

Warr, Mark. 1998. "Life-Course Transitions and Desistance from Crime." *Criminology* 36(2):183–216.

Warr, Mark. 2002. *Companions in Crime: The Social Aspects of Criminal Conduct.* New York, NY: Cambridge University Press.

Warr, Mark and Mark Stafford. 1991. "The Influence of Delinquent Peers: What They Think or What They Do?" *Criminology* 29(4):851–66.

Wasserman, Stanley, John Scott, and Peter J. Carrington. 2005. "Introduction." Pp. 1–7 in *Models and Methods in Social Network Analysis,* edited by P. J. Carrington, J. Scott, and S. Wasserman. Cambridge, MA: Cambridge University Press.

Wasserman, Stanley and Katherine Faust. 1994. *Social Network Analysis: Methods and Applications. Structural Analysis in the Social Sciences Vol. 8.* Cambridge, UK: Cambridge University Press.

Wechsler, Henry, Jae Eun Lee, Meichun Kuo, Mark Seibring, Toben F. Nelson, and Hang Lee. 2002. "Trends in College Binge Drinking During a Period of Increased Prevention Efforts: Findings from Four Harvard School of Public Health College Alcohol Study Surveys: 1993–2001." *Journal of American College Health* 50(5):203–17.

Weerman, Frank. 2011. "Delinquent Peers in Context: A Longitudinal Network Analysis of Selection and Influence Effects." *Criminology* 49(1):253–86.

Wentzel, Kathryn R., Alice Donlan, and Danette Morrison. 2012. "Peer Relationships and Social-Motivational Processes." Pp. 79–108 in *Peer Relationships and Adjustment at School,* edited by A. M. Ryan and G. W. Ladd. Charlotte, NC: Information Age Publishing.

Wentzel, Kathryn R., Carolyn M. Barry, and Kathryn A. Caldwell. 2004. "Friendships in Middle School: Influences on Motivation and School Adjustment." *Journal of Educational Psychology* 96(2):195–203.

Wentzel, Kathryn R. and Steven R. Asher. 1995. "The Academic Lives of Neglected, Rejected, Popular, and Controversial Children." *Child Development* 66(3):754–63.

Wiatrowski, Michael D., David B. Griswold, and Mary K. Roberts. 1981. "Social Control Theory and Delinquency." *American Sociological Review* 46(5):525–41.

Wing, Rena R. and Robert W. Jeffery. 1999. "Benefits of Recruiting Participants with Friends and Increasing Social Support for Weight Loss and Maintenance." *Journal of Consulting and Clinical Psychology* 67(1):132–38.

Yablonsky, Lewis. 1963. *The Violent Gang.* New York, NY: Macmillan.

Young, Jacob T. N. and Frank Weerman. 2013. "Delinquency as a Consequence of Misperception: Overestimation of Friends' Delinquent Behavior and Mechanisms of Social Influence." *Social Problems* 60(3):334–56.

Youniss, James and Jacqueline Smollar. 1985. *Adolescent Relations with Mother, Fathers, and Friends.* Chicago, IL: University of Chicago Press.

INDEX